101 Career Questions Answered on Working with Special Needs Children

By:

Tammi Reynolds

The 101 Series
ISBN # 0-9788069-6-4
© Copyright 2007 Tammi Reynolds
All Rights Reserved
Printed in the U.S.A.
www.laurellanepublishing.com
Creative Director: Jason McCloy
Cover Art: Jaime Polasky

About The 101 Series...

You've got career questions?
We've got career answers!

Every release in The 101 Series takes the questions that you've asked about a *specific* career field and gets them answered by experienced professionals.

Find out the education you absolutely need. Get information from insiders about important skills. Prepare for interviews and learn more about what it's like growing your career.

Whether you're just starting to think about college or already a member of the workforce, The 101 Series delivers straight answers to your important questions.

How to use this book...

Every book in The 101 Series is easy to use. Read it from cover to cover or open to any page and just let curiosity be your guide. Any way you choose to use this guide, you can trust that the information comes from experienced, working professionals answering the questions you have asked and the ones you didn't know you needed to ask.

Check out these other books in

The 101 Series
at
www.laurellanepublishing.com

Questions Answered on *Your Career*!
Working for Nonprofits & Interest Groups
Being a Medical Billing Specialist
Being a Naturopathic Practitioner
Working in the Hospitality Industry
Working as an Information Technology Specialist
Being a High School Teacher
Being a College Professor
and
Many More to Come!

Disclaimer:

This guide covers basic information for those considering or just starting a career in a field related to working with special needs children. The information in this text is current as of the date of printing. However, information, especially certification requirements, website or contact information, can change rapidly.

Please check for the latest information through applicable organizations. Laurel Lane Publishing and the author accept no responsibility for any adverse outcomes from undetected errors, omissions, or outdated material, or for the reader's misinterpretation of the information contained herein.

MAIN INDEX

Your Questions Answered on...

THE BASICS.. **Page 5**

DEFINING 'SPECIAL NEEDS'.................................. **Page 20**

THERAPY IN ACTION.. **Page 41**

TOOLS OF THE TRADE... **Page 75**

THERAPY: ACTIVITIES AND STRATEGIES........... **Page 96**

THERAPY IN DIFFERENT SETTINGS..................... **Page 123**

PAPERWORK AND TRAINING................................. **Page 134**

REFERENCE.. **Page 141**

Your Questions Answered on...

THE BASICS

1. What is a therapist? What is a TSS? **Page # 6**

2. What qualifications does a therapist need? **Page # 8**

3. What is a case manager? **Page # 9**

4. What qualifications does a case manager need? **Page # 10**

5. What is a behavioral specialist? **Page # 11**

6. What qualifications does a behavioral specialist need? **Page # 12**

7. What types of conflicts arise within a treatment team? **Page # 13**

8. What are the benefits in working with special needs children? **Page # 15**

9. What treatment program is used most frequently? **Page # 16**

10. What is the Relationship Development Intervention Program? **Page # 17**

11. How much do the different positions related to working with special needs children get paid? **Page # 18**

QUESTION 1

What is a therapist? What is a TSS?

TSS stands for, "therapeutic staff support worker." This staff member works one on one with children and adolescents who are behaviorally challenged or emotionally disturbed. Therapeutic support staff members are typically affiliated with a process called **Wraparound.** The main function of a TSS worker is to help the child (usually referred to as the 'client') learn to navigate through everyday situations without behavioral problems. The leading demand for therapeutic staff support is with autistic children.

Therapists deliver services in homes, schools and communities. These individuals are responsible for implementing the treatment plan as well as documenting the child's progress. Through the use of behavioral interventions and strategies the TSS helps the child transition and helps him tolerate his environment. Each client has a treatment plan that specifies areas of concern. These usually involve social, behavioral and emotional elements.

TSS as part of a team - The therapeutic staff support works collaboratively with a team. The team consists of the family, the behavior specialist, and case manager. The family identifies areas of concern and the behavior specialist develops a treatment plan. The case manager assigns therapeutic staff support to the case and schedules shifts for therapy. A shift typically spans three hours.

TSS putting treatment into action - The role of the therapeutic support staff is crucial to the child's treatment. The TSS is the "hands-on" member of the team who puts the treatment plan into action. The behavior specialist supervises the therapeutic support staff on site and during weekly meetings. However, the therapeutic support staff primarily works on-site with the client without supervision.

TSS as a communicator - Communication is essential in a team environment, so the therapist is responsible for recording the client's progress and keeping accurate data. This data is used to measure the child's progress and determine what changes need to be made in the treatment plan. The therapeutic staff support also relays information about the client's progress to the family and explains behavioral interventions and strategies for the family to use. The idea is to gradually make therapy unnecessary by helping the family develop management skills independently.

The position is not tedious. A therapist may work with a family for a few months or a few years and a therapist generally works with a number of clients so the atmosphere is always changing. Since treatment is provided in the home, schools and within the community, a therapist will also find themselves working in a number of different environments, alongside a number of other professionals.

Now, you might be wondering ....

2. What qualifications does a therapist need? **Page # 8**
3. What is a case manager? **Page # 9**
4. What qualifications does a case manager need? **Page # 10**
5. What is a behavioral specialist? **Page # 11**
6. What qualifications does a behavioral specialist need? **Page # 12**
7. What types of conflicts arise within a treatment team? **Page # 13**
8. What are the benefits in working with special needs children? **Page # 15**
9. What treatment program is used most frequently? **Page # 16**
11. How much do the different positions related to working with special needs children get paid? **Page # 18**
12. What are autism & PDD? **Page # 21**
95. Where are some websites where I can learn more about Wraparound? **Page # 152**
96. What are some different roles that I can take in a career spent working with special needs children? **Page # 153**

A Little on Professional Titles

In this question, we covered what a TSS does. *Therapeutic Support Specialist* is a term that is specific to the **Wraparound program**, which is covered in greater detail throughout this guide. In some other programs, the title *Mobile Therapist* would be used to describe a professional working in a similar environment with comparable goals.

Throughout your career you will come across numerous titles, many of which you never heard of while in college or during a training program. Your first few years in a field after school should be spent learning not just your job, but getting an idea for the structure of the professional field, who does what and how they all work together to reach a common goal.

QUESTION 2: What qualifications does a therapist need?

A therapist usually needs to have a four year degree in social work, psychology or a related field. Agencies are quite flexible about the applicant's degree since extensive training is provided. Experience working with children is usually necessary. Agencies seek applicants who have experience with child development and childhood disorders, but again, training is extensive and ongoing.

Clearances are required for these positions. The applicant needs to get a criminal background check and child abuse clearance per OAPSA and Child Protective Services Act. A therapist also must have a valid driver's license and a clean driving record.

Aside from general education requirements, there are specific characteristics that agencies look for in the on-site therapist. The staff member should be able to work independently and decisively. No one is there to tell a therapist what to do, so it is essential that this professional is able to organize and implement therapy without supervision. Because the therapist works independently, good communication skills are very important. The family and the rest of the team rely on the them to effectively convey the child's progress and assure that the child's needs are being met.

A therapist should also demonstrate an ability to develop an appropriate relationship with children and adolescents. A good therapist has an understanding of child and adolescent development as well as knowledge about developmental disorders, especially autism. When working with this delicate population, it is important that a therapist remain calm and organized. Much of the time they are serving as models for the child with regards to appropriate actions.

Therapy is often held in a variety of settings. Some hours are spent in schools, some are in the community and some are in homes. Therapy may also be scheduled during evenings and weekends, so a staff member can fill hours while attending college, raising a family or working at another job.

The Wraparound program brings therapy to the client. This is where you'll generally find a TSS and the structure of the program can be very flexible, offering numerous opportunities.

Now, you might be wondering ....

9. What treatment program is used most frequently? **Page # 16**

96. What are some different roles that I can take in a career spent working with special needs children? **Page # 153**

What is a case manager?

QUESTION 3

The title of, 'Case Manager,' has different meanings according to the type of program being described. In a Wraparound program, which is a program that involves numerous agencies and is primarily geared towards providing services for a special needs child directly in the home, school and community, a case manager is responsible for coordinating care. This professional works with family members, school officials and others to determine therapeutic needs, schedule appointments and move care forward. The case manager will also meet with the therapist and behavioral specialist to review treatment objectives and make certain that goals are being met.

Outside of the Wraparound program (and other programs that focus primarily on autism treatment), a case worker is akin to a probation officer. In the juvenile justice system, this professional is responsible for meeting with and guiding the child through the system.

If you are thinking about a career working with special needs children, you would want to determine exactly what that means to you. Throughout this book, we focus on working with children diagnosed with autism and Pervasive Development Disorders. In this instance, working as a case manager would mean coordinating services (meeting with school officials, families and other staff, to see that treatment is being conducted and on course, as well as managing therapists and other social services workers). This position offers the least amount of direct contact with the children, but is instrumental in guaranteeing that services are provided. It is not unusual for a case manager in a Wraparound program to have begun as a therapist and then moved into the more administrative role, managing the treatment of many individuals, but with less direct contact. Outside of Wraparound programs, where children live onsite (such as at a residential facility, special school or hospital), any position in the administration of the facility would be comparable to case management work.

The important thing to understand is that there are multiple roles available in this field. Case managers work more in the coordination of treatment, while a behavioral specialist controls the actual nature of that treatment and the therapist delivers the treatment. Taking the time to think of which role suits you is a good way to make certain that you work towards the position that compliments you.

Now, you might be wondering ....

1. What is a therapist? What is a TSS? **Page # 6**
2. What qualifications does a therapist need? **Page # 8**
4. What qualifications does a case manager need? **Page # 10**

QUESTION 4
What qualifications does a case manager need?

Generally, a case manager will hold a BA or BS in Psychology, Social Work or a related field. It is not uncommon for employers to require two years of experience working with the disabled, elderly or children, in order to take a position within a Wraparound program.

In addition to these requirements, many states and employers require their case managers to be certified. This means holding the CCM credential (certified case manager). In order to receive this credential, you must apply to sit for an exam given by the *Commission for Case Manager Certification*. To even sit for the exam a number of criteria must be met, including sufficient work experience, educational requirements and after certification, continuing professional education requirements. You can learn more about the CCM at: **www.ccmcertification.org**

CMAC - Case Manager Administrator Certification - The CMAC is another professional certification that may be required in addition to your education and work experience. It is granted through the *Center for Case Management*. Requirements include passing an exam along with a combined number of years work experience and educational degrees. The certification also carries continuing educational requirements. You can learn more at: **www.cfcm.com**.

Certifications are an important part of a career. Not only do they test your current knowledge, the organizations that monitor certifications hold important roles within a specific professional community. They verify experience and support a professional's continued education. Employers often value their certified professionals for their dedication to improving their skills and knowledge.

Now, you might be wondering ....

1. What is a therapist? **Page # 6**
2. What qualifications does a therapist need? **Page # 8**
5. What is a behavioral specialist? **Page # 11**
6. What qualifications does a behavioral specialist need? **Page # 14**
9. What treatment program is used most frequently? **Page # 16**
12. What are autism & PDD? **Page # 21**
91. Where can I find employment opportunities? **Page # 146**
96. What are some different roles that I can take in a career spent working with special needs children? **Page # 153**

What is a behavioral specialist?

QUESTION 5

Normally supervised by a psychologist, the behavioral specialist is responsible for developing and making changes to a treatment plan. By assessing the child, meeting with other team members and reviewing data collected by the therapist during regular sessions, the behavioral specialist works to develop the original treatment plan and make changes throughout the course of therapy to help progress the client towards established goals. While the case manager handles administrative needs, the behaviorist decides on the specifics of the actual treatment that is then carried out by the therapist on-site.

Generally, it is the therapist's responsibility to conduct the on-site interventions, carrying out the treatment plan as established by the team. While conducting therapeutic interventions, the therapist also records data regarding the client's behavior. Records are kept for everything from how well the client progresses through a short drill, to the length and specific nature of a temper tantrum. The behavioral specialist is responsible for interpreting this data and making changes to the treatment plan in accordance.

The behavior specialist also takes direction from the client's psychologist. In the case of a hospitalized client, the specialist would be guided by a Unit Director (or psychologist).

Within the dynamics of the team, the behavior specialist's responsibilities are related to data evaluation, treatment decisions and also, frequent on-site supervision of therapists to make certain that they are following necessary protocol when meeting with clients. The specialist may also make on-site visits when obstacles arise that the TSS is not able to handle on his or her own.

Now, you might be wondering ....

1. What is a therapist? What is a TSS? **Page # 6**
2. What qualifications does a therapist need? **Page # 8**
6. What qualifications does a behavioral specialist need? **Page # 14**
9. What treatment program is used most frequently? **Page # 16**
12. What are autism & PDD? **Page # 21**
29. What is behavior? **Page # 44**
84. What are supervision meetings and why are they important? **Page # 136**
96. What are some different roles that I can take in a career spent working with special needs children? **Page # 153**

QUESTION 6

What qualifications does a behavioral specialist need?

The requirements for a behavior specialist can vary according to the agency that hires them. However, a behavior specialist is usually required to have a master's degree in psychology, counseling or a related field. It's not uncommon for a behaviroal specialist to find a position with a master's degree in education.

It is possible for a behavior specialist to find a position with a bachelor's degree. The one major problem in this situation is that without a master's degree, they are unable to oversee monthly supervisions. Monthly supervisions are when the specialist visits clients with the therapist to gauge how successfully the treatment plan is being put into action. Being unable to attend supervisions can be a major hurdle to finding a position because it seriously detracts from the professional's effectiveness when filling this role.

There are two main certifications that can help a person to find a position as a behavioral specialist. They are the *Preventive Intervention Course Certification (PIC)* and the *Nonviolent Crisis Intervention (NCI)*. Nonviolent Crisis Intervention (NCI) is administered through the Crisis Prevention Institute, Inc. You can learn more about the organization and certification at www.crisisprevention.com.

Both of these certifications are usually worked into the educational requirements for any master's program related to health services and most organizations make them requirements for employment. In some cases, depending on the agency's need, you will be able to work on earning certifications in these areas after being hired, but this is highly unlikely.

Now, you might be wondering ....

7. What types of conflicts arise within a treatment team? **Page # 13**
8. What are the benefits in working with special needs children? **Page # 15**
9. What treatment program is used most frequently? **Page # 16**
11. How much do the different positions related to working with special needs children get paid? **Page # 18**
12. What are autism & PDD? **Page # 21**
28. What is applied behavioral analysis? **Page # 42**
84. What are supervision meetings and why are they important? **Page # 136**
91. Where can I find employment opportunities? **Page # 146**

What types of conflicts arise within a treatment team?

QUESTION 7

In a Wraparound program, the case manager, therapist and behaviorist work together to form a treatment team. The family, school administration and teachers are also team members, but they change as clients change. This constant change in peripheral team members is normally the source of major conflict, because they tend to have a problem understanding how much time must go into studying the behaviors of a child before anything becomes determined and treatment is altered. In short, therapy is systematic and takes time. The most common problems arise when this is not properly communicated to family members, teachers and school administrators.

The best advice for budding therapists to take is to never give advice. It is very common for family members and teachers to ask therapists for explanations about behavior. Understanding the reasons behind the behaviors of special needs children is very difficult. It takes an entire team of experienced professionals, gathering evidence in the form of organized data and the review of that data, to begin to accomplish this.

To illustrate how problems arise from stepping outside of the correct process, consider the following example. A client has a tantrum everyday at the same time and the family members want an explanation for this. The following paragraphs cover areas where stepping outside of the therapeutic process causes problems:

The functions of behavior are never immediately apparent: If the therapeutic staff support worker witnesses a child's tantrum and says, "Don't give in. She just wants to get out of work," and the team finds that the child gets hungry at that time everyday, the advice was simply wrong. Wrong advice undermines the family's faith in the treatment team, making it much more difficult to help the child.

The consequences of a behavior are almost never consistent: A child who has a tantrum in the presence of his grandmother will not experience the same result as what would occur by throwing a tantrum in the presence of the father or brother. Part of the therapist's job is to watch how these behaviors play out. The therapist needs to record the consequences of the behavior in different situations. Until this is done, you can't begin to understand the behavior and until you understand the behavior and have consulted with the team, there is no sound advice to give.

Wraparound is a process: Any therapy, for that matter, is a process. There are no quick-fixes. Conflicts arise when anyone involved in the treatment does not understand how lengthy this process can be or everything involved in it.

Consistent Communication is essential. Inconsistent communication causes problems: One therapist on a case may tell a family that a child exhibits a behavior because they are hungry. Another may tell the family that the child exhibits this behavior to get out of work. This type of inconsistent communication undermines the team and makes it more difficult to facilitate treatment.

Wraparound is child-specific and clinical: A functional analysis needs to be completed before determining appropriate steps to dealing with specific behaviors. Information should be collected and the behavior specialist has to have an opportunity to develop a strategy to address any behavior.

A functional analysis is completed in steps and the members of the child's treatment team, including the family, work as a unit. Once the team has targeted the problem behavior, the members of the team begin taking objective, measurable data that includes the antecedent, the behavior itself and the consequences for the behavior. After enough data is collected, the team determines possible functions of the behavior and the behavior specialist develops strategies that the treatment team uses to address the behavior. Premature advice can undermine the team and break down communication. If a behavior is consistently interfering with the child's everyday activities, it needs to be addressed, but it needs to be addressed systematically.

Now, you might be wondering ....

28. What is applied behavioral analysis? **Page # 42**
29. What is behavior? **Page # 44**
54. What is an ABC chart? **Page # 86**
72. What are some strategies for teaching replacement behaviors? **Page # 113**
70. What are some strategies for working with families? **Page # 110**
95. Where are some websites where I can learn more about Wraparound? **Page # 152**

Common problems

In the last section we learned that the most frequent problem encountered by a treatment team involves poor communication with families, school administration and teachers. This is why excellent communication skills are such a major part of this profession. If you decide to take a role working with special needs children, develop your communication skills. Learn how to talk with people and deliver easy to understand, effective, statements. This skill will make you valuable in this professional field and help you to provide excellent treatment to deserving individuals.

What are the benefits in working with special needs children?

QUESTION 8

Being a member of a treatment team has been a challenging and rewarding career. I have met incredibly talented and knowledgeable professionals in this field. I have had an opportunity to work with many different teachers, each with a unique approach to teaching and each with a unique affinity to their students. Just getting the opportunity to be exposed to so many different professionals and educational styles is definitely a major benefit.

Working with families: I have also worked with many families, each with their individual dynamics and personalities. As a therapist and constant student of behavior, this has taught me much about families and people in general. On a more personal level, you get to take a role in the lives of many different people and do something with lasting impact for them.

Developing teaching skills: As I learned more and more about the autism spectrum of disorders through this profession, I gained a deeper insight into how we all learn, how we all develop and how we all relate to each other. I have a new perspective on learning and motivation that is applicable as much to teaching an elementary class as to working in a therapeutic environment. In addition to this hands-on experience, the continuing educational classes I had the opportunity to attend provided me with a wealth of valuable knowledge. These classes are applicable to many fields.

Learning teamwork: The importance of teamwork was never so clear to me until I worked as a therapist. I am continuously amazed at how much progress a team can make when working in synchronicity.

Flexible schedule: This career catered to my schedule when I took graduate classes. It was flexible enough to allow me time to plan my wedding, and it literally revolved around my schedule as I became a mother for the first time. A full-time employee can choose to work long days in exchange for more days off, or she can work short days throughout the week. A part-time staff member can work with the case manager to create a schedule that fits the therapists needs and the needs of the families.

Personal benefits: Nothing in my experience as a therapist has benefited me more than the many children who have touched my life over the years. I am fortunate to have experienced the struggles and the great victories as well as the small victories in my work.

Now, you might be wondering ....

100. I think I want to work with special needs children, where should I start? **Page #159**

QUESTION 9
Which treatment program is used most frequently? What is Wraparound?

Wraparound services are the most common in the United States for special needs children living outside of a residential treatment facility. The program is designed to literally *wrap around the family*. Before the development of Wraparound, autistic children or adolescents would normally be removed from the community and institutionalized. This could mean a hospital for autistic children or a juvenile hall for emotionally disturbed children who have had trouble with authorities. Wraparound brings treatment to the child, teaching them, with the assitance of teachers, parents and community members, how to function successfully in their natural social environment. The following are some important points about Wraparound:

Wraparound is a process - Though they are temporary, these programs are designed to bring therapy to the client's natural environment. The program provides practical on-site interventions and activities that are applicable to the family's everyday life. Therapy may be held in the home, school or community, depending on the child's specific needs. Bringing therapy to the client's natural environment helps the family incorporate management strategies into their daily routines seamlessly.

Wraparound is a relatively new concept - The Brownsdale programs, developed in Canada by John Brown and his colleagues in the sixties and seventies, brought individualized treatment to clients. In the United States, Karl Dennis developed similar programs under Kaleidoscope. Kaleidoscope began delivering individual therapy to clients in 1975. The Alaska Youth Initiative is another program that was developed in 1985 and founded by John VanDenBerg. This organization focused on bringing services to children who would normally be sent out of state for therapy. Through this program, children and adolescents who lived in Alaska could receive services at home rather than being sent to institutions out of state. Many states followed VanDenBerg's design and agencies like Alaska Youth Initiative emerged. To find out more about agencies that provide services in your state, reference **www.autismlink.com**. This site has listings of organizations under each state.

Wraparound is community based and family-centered - These services focus on the strengths and needs of the family.

Wraparound is still evolving - It is an exciting time to be involved in such a dynamic practice, and there are many opportunities available for the right people.

Now, you might be wondering ....

94. What are some methods for autism treatment aside from ABA? **Page # 150**
95. Where are some websites where I can learn more about Wraparound? **Page # 152**

What is the Relationship Development Intervention Program?

QUESTION 10

Therapists who work with an RDI program are trained and certified in Relationship Development Intervention. RDI was developed by Steve Gutstein and is a relatively new program that focuses on social development. A child who receives RDI services works with a professional RDI consultant. The Relationship Development Intervention program is the child's primary program. The RDI program can be supplemented with other interventions, but the focus is relationship development.

RDI resembles Applied Behavior Analysis in some ways:

1. RDI is parent-based. The family is an integral part of the program.
2. RDI uses objectives to structure the sessions.
3. The RDI consultant uses interventions to help the child attain objectives. The consultant is trained to use specific strategies to engage the child.
4. RDI is clinical and objective. The child is diagnosed with a developmental disorder and the program is set up according to a plan.
5. The RDI consultant collects data on a daily basis.
6. The child's progress in the program is reviewed periodically and revised accordingly.
7. RDI breaks social interaction down into steps. Once the child masters one step, he moves on to the next.

Relationship Development Intervention is a step-by-step process that eventually leads to a child interacting with a number of different people. The program begins one-on-one and progresses into group sessions. The child learns to interpret nonverbal social cues, like gestures and facial expressions. As the sessions continue, the child learns the concept of sharing and develops empathy and awareness of others.

Most therapists are not Relationship Development Intervention consultants. In order to become an RDI consultant, a therapist has to complete training and certification through the program. It is good to explore other programs and educate yourself about as many as you can. Some agencies decide to integrate RDI into their services, making it necessary for their therapists to become certified. A similar program that focuses on relationship development is called the Son-Rise program.

Now, you might be wondering ....

9. What treatment program is used most frequently? **Page # 16**
28. What is applied behavioral analysis? **Page # 42**
94. What are some methods for autism treatment aside from ABA? **Page # 150**

QUESTION 11

How much do the different positions related to working with special needs children get paid?

As a rule, earnings can vary greatly even among people working in the same positions. Things such as number of years experience, region, educational achievements and special certifications all play a part in determining the exact pay that a professional will receive. The following figures give you an idea of the range of pay for different positions related to working with special needs children:

Therapist (Therapeutic Support Specialist or TSS) - Typically, a TSS or on-site therapist will earn between $10 and $18 an hour. Many therapists work part time, arranging their schedule around school or other responisbilities, making this the position with the greatest amount of flexibility.

Case Manager - There is a pretty wide range with regards to pay for a case manager. Normally, you can expect to make anywhere from $35,000 to $65,000. The state and city you work in can play a major part in determining pay for this position.

Behavior Specialist - Behavior specialist's also have a wide range in pay. These professionals can earn anywhere from $28,000 to $60,000 or more. In this instance, the state and city where you work, your educational achievements and the organization that you work for all determine your pay. Experience is another important factor.

Other positions - Throughout this book we focus pretty heavily on the three roles of therapist, case manager and behavior specialist. There are plenty of other types of positions that a person could take related to working with special needs children. For example, residential facilities where autistic children live full time employ people to manage the children within their residence. Hospitals employ special orderlies. Special schools employ teachers and teaching assistants. Interestingly enough, all the different roles you can take somehow tie into the three we have focused on. A special education teacher will need many of the same skills that a therapist has because they both spend the greatest amount of time interacting directly with the children. Case managers for a Wraparound program will have many of the same responsibilities as administrators in a residential program. The behaviorist deals with the way that treatment is designed in a Wraparound program in much the same way that a person in a similar role in a hospital or residential facility would.

The best way to approach understanding the ranges in pay and how they relate to different types of positions in different environments is to think according to responsibilities. If you are managing treatment, then you'll probably earn within the case manager's range. If you are delivering treatment, expect to earn within the therapist's range. The same goes for working as a behaviorist. Just remember, there are differences in every situation. Pay and responsibilities vary.

Now, you might be wondering ....

96. What are some different roles that I can take in a career spent working with special needs children? **Page # 153**
97. What education is required for the different roles you can take working with special needs children? **Page # 155**
98. What are some related fields that I can pursue after getting experience working with special needs children? **Page # 156**
99. What are some notable organizations related to the history of working with special needs children? **Page # 158**
100. I think I want to work with special needs children, where should I start? **Page # 159**
101. What's next? **Page # 160**

Money, money, money...

One of the biggest factors that lead people to choose one career over another is the pay. You need money to pay for your home, food, clothing and everything else you need to survive. However, it is very wise to take other factors into consideration.

If you notice in the last section, the pay ranges vary. A case manager's pay can vary as much as thirty thousand dollars a year, depending on where they work, their experience and credentials, the demands of the job and a number of other factors.

Virtually every type of job has a variance with pay. Most students and new graduates look at these and almost automatically assume they will earn the median or middle pay range (if not more). In reality, as a new graduate, you should expect to earn closer to the lowest pay grade (unless if you have an advanced degree). There are exceptions, but you want to take this into consideration. Regardless of what career you decide to work in, always expect that the highest pay on any published pay-grade scale is going to go to the people with most experience (meaning the ones that got the most experience in that professional field).

DEFINING 'SPECIAL NEEDS'

Your Questions Answered on...

12. What are autism & PDD? **Page # 21**

13. What are the Pervasive Development Disorders? **Page # 22**

14. What are the similarities and differences between Asperger's syndrome and autism? **Page #24**

15. How do autistic children suffer from body awareness deficiencies? **Page # 26**

16. What sensory issues affect autistic & PDD children? **Page # 27**

17. What are tactile, vestibular and proprioceptive systems? **Page # 28**

18. How do self-stimulatory behaviors involve the senses? **Page # 29**

19. What is perseveration? **Page # 31**

20. What is echolalia? **Page # 32**

21. How does an autistic child use echolalia to communicate? **Page # 34**

22. What is theory of mind? **Page # 35**

23. What is functional language? **Page # 36**

24. What is non-verbal imitation? **Page # 37**

25. What deficiencies do autistic children have with auditory processing? **Page # 38**

26. What are executive function deficits? **Page # 39**

27. How do autistic and PDD children process language? **Page # 40**

What are autism and PDD?

QUESTION 12

Autism is a mysterious condition that falls under a broad spectrum of symptoms. Individuals diagnosed within the spectrum have varying interests, abilities and severity. The number of individuals diagnosed within the autism spectrum has dramatically increased in the past decade. In the early 1990's, one in 2500 children was diagnosed with autism. That number has increased to as many as one in 166.

The affliction is fundamentally a neurological disorder. It is a condition that emerges within the first three years of a child's life and the cause is unknown. Some theories state that autism is developed through the environment; others maintain that it is primarily a genetic disorder. Boys are more apt to have autism than girls, but autism is not prevalent in any particular race or social class.

Children with autism have difficulty with social interaction, communication, attention and behavior. With regards to social interaction, autistic children tend to lack eye contact and also tend to show a lack of emotion and a lack of interest in others. Most autistic children do not respond to their names. Their play activities are unusual and ritualistic. Another very common trait for autistic children is to engage in self-stimulatory behaviors. Hand flapping and perseveration (constant repetition of words) are the common examples for repetitive self-stimularory behaviors for autistic children.

Autism is a pervasive developmental disorder. Pervasive developmental disorder (PDD) relates to a group of disorders that involve developmental delays in communication and social skills. PDD is not a single disorder but a group of disorders that have similar characteristics. Pervasive developmental disorder is also referred to as autism spectrum disorder. Children diagnosed with PDD have difficulty relating to others in social situations. Just as the name suggests, a pervasive developmental disorder is subtle, resulting in gradually increasing harm. A pervasive developmental disorder has an effect on nearly every aspect of the child's life, as well as the family's life. It is difficult to recognize pervasive developmental disorders because different children develop at different rates. Some children begin using language early, others take a much longer time to learn those skills.

Now, you might be wondering ....

14. What are the similarities and differences between Asperger's syndrome and autism? **Page # 24**
27. How do autistic and other PDD children process language? **Page # 40**
92. Where can I find current information related to autism studies? **Page # 147**

QUESTION 13: What are the pervasive developmental disorders?

There are five pervasive developmental disorders. Therapists can work with children having any one of the five disorders, but it is most common to work with children diagnosed with PDD-NOS, autism and Asperger's Syndrome.

Children who are diagnosed with PDD-NOS or Asperger's syndrome are usually high-functioning. Children diagnosed with autism vary in ability. Rett syndrome and childhood disintegrative disorder are more rare and severe.

If you are interested in learning more about diagnostic criteria for PDD, you can visit **www.childbrain.com**. Below are the five Pervasive Development Disorders and a quick description of the diagnostic criteria:

1. Pervasive Developmental Disorder, Not Otherwise Specified (PDD-NOS)

This diagnosis is used when the child has a significant impairment in social interactions, or verbal and nonverbal communication skills, but the criteria are not met for a specific pervasive developmental disorder as outlined in the Diagnostic and Stastical Manual of Mental Disorders (DSM IV).

2. Autistic Disorder

A child diagnosed with autism exhibits six characteristics from the categories of *social interaction*, *communication impairments* and *stereotyped patterns of behavior*. The child must have at least two social interaction impairments and at least one delay or impairment in communication development. They must also exhibit stereotyped patterns of behavior, interests and activities. A good example of stereotypical autistic behavior is hand flapping. The child would also have difficulty with imaginative play and social language.

3. Asperger's Disorder (or Asperger Syndrome)

A child diagnosed with Asperger's exhibits at least two impairments regarding social interactions. The child engages in stereotyped patterns of behavior, interests and activities and the child has significant impairment of social functioning, but does not exhibit a significant delay in language. A child diagnosed with Asperger's Syndrome does not exhibit a delay in cognitive development or self-help skills. The child is curious about his environment and is able to adjust, except in social situations.

4. Rett's Disorder (or Rett Syndrome)

Rett Syndrome is a disorder that is almost exclusive to females. Males that have the syndrome die before or shortly after birth.

These children develop normally until between five and forty-eight months of age. During the onset of Rett Syndrome, the child significantly loses hand skills and replaces them with stereotyped hand movements, like flapping. The child has poor coordination and serious psychomotor delays. Language and communication development would also be severely impaired.

5. Childhood Disintegrative Disorder

A child diagnosed with childhood disintegrative disorder exhibits normal development for at least the first two years of life. The child has verbal and nonverbal communication skills, social skills, adaptive skills and play skills, but loses these suddenly in at least two areas. The child may lose language, social, play, or motor skills. The child may lose bowel or bladder control. The loss of the skills must be significant enough to impair at least two of the following areas: social interaction, communication and/or appropriate play and mannerisms.

Now, you might be wondering ....

14. What are the similarities and differences between Asperger's syndrome and autism? **Page # 24**
27. How do autistic and PDD children process language? **Page # 40**
28. What is applied behavioral analysis? **Page # 42**
89. What books are available to help me learn more about working with special needs children? **Page # 143**
90. What are some important moments in the history of autism treatment? **Page # 144**

Keeping up with research and development

Autism and PDD research are at full throttle in virtually every major college in the country (and many other countries). If you plan on developing an excellent career working with special needs children, you'll want to keep up with new developments.

Some interesting programs include the studies being conducted at Yale (www.med.yale.edu), King's College London (www.kcl.ac.uk) and at Cambridge (www.autismresearchcentre.com).

QUESTION 14

What are the similarities and differences between Asperger's Syndrome and autism?

The characteristics of autism and Asperger's Syndrome are very similar, enough so that the terms are often interchanged. At the start of my career, I had difficulty separating the two disorders because they shared so many characteristics. The following are criteria for diagnosis according to the Diagnositc and Statistical Manual for Mental Disorders (DSM IV).

Similarities include:

At least two of the following:

1. Social impairment in nonverbal behaviors.

Examples of social impairment in nonverbal behaviors are the absence of gestures or body positioning in relation to others. Autistic and Asperger's children also tend to not have facial expressions or they are inappropriate.

2. Failure to create relationships with peers.

3. Does not share interests and enjoyment with others.

Both Asperger's and autistic children usually will not point to objects of interest. They will not show these objects or share them with others. The children also fail to show pride in achievements.

4. Does not reciprocate socially or emotionally.

The autistic and Asperger's child usually will not empathize with others or respond to social questions.

At least one of the following:

1. Preoccupation with restricted patterns of interests.

Children suffering from these afflictions may become fascinated with a particular subject. This interest is usually intensely focused, interfering with the child's daily life.

2. Engaging in strict routines or rituals.

Routines and rituals can play a major role in the life of autistic and Asperger's children.

They are normally very rigid with regards to their routines, though the actions serve no purpose.

3. Repetitive movements of body parts.

These children are not easily redirected from repeating certain movements. They often ignore their environment.

4. Preoccupation with parts of objects.

Differences - Both autism and Asperger's share the characteristics listed above. However, the disorders also have differences. **The major difference lies in communication.** This includes communication in all forms.

Differences include:

An autistic child exhibits at least one of the following:

1. Does not use language.

Autistic children may not speak, use facial expressions or gestures to communicate.

2. Children who speak do not use language appropriately.

An autistic child may not initiate or reciprocate conversation. Children who are diagnosed within the autism spectrum of disorders (PDD) vary in abilities and interests. Children with Asperger's Syndrome are often very advanced in their ability to use language (often more advanced than peers that develop according to a normal timeline). For quite awhile, this one difference made it difficult to get help for children suffering from Asperger's.

Now, you might be wondering ....

16. What sensory issues affect autistic & PDD children? **Page # 27**
27. How do autistic and PDD children process language? **Page # 40**
28. What is applied behavioral analysis? **Page # 42**
29. What is behavior? **Page # 44**
89. What books are available to help me learn more about working with special needs children? **Page # 143**
90. What are some important moments in the history of autism treatment? **Page # 144**
100. I think I want to work with special needs children, where should I start? **Page # 159**

QUESTION 15
How do autistic children suffer from body awareness deficiencies?

Many autistic children do not have a sense of self in relation to their environment. Therapists frequently experience cases where children have difficulty identifying their own body parts. This lack of body awareness leads to significant problems that lie in the child's inability to process sensory information appropriately.

Body awareness deficiencies result from the child's inability to take in or, "block out," sensory input. They may not know what to focus on or what to filter out. Sensory problems are common in autism and have been described in a number of different ways. One person may feel disconnected from his surroundings and another may feel completely dispersed in his surroundings. One person may crave hugs while another may be overwhelmed by touch.

Sensory issues interfere with the individual's ability to navigate through everyday situations and result in accidents with the potential of physical harm. The child may tend to run into objects or be prone to trip. A therapist addresses these probelms with sensory integration activities and Applied Behavioral Analysis drills that are designed to help the child cope with sensory issues.

One such activity is called, 'receptive body parts drills.' The child is given the instruction (stimulus or SD), "touch," and then the body part that is being targeted in the drill. For example, the therapist may say, "Touch feet." After the child masters this phase, the drill advances further. The child is then directed to reference his own body parts, making it necessary for the child to acknowledge himself. Typically, you work with a body part the child can see, such as the feet. As the drills progress, therapists will usually work their way up to the head.

Over time, the repetition of these exercises lead to the child developing a sense of their self in relation to environment. This is a significant achievement for autistic children.

Now, you might be wondering ....

39. How do drills adhere to the treatment plan? **Page # 60**
40. How do drills relate to applied behavioral analysis? **Page # 62**
41. What is a discrete stimulus or SD? **Page # 64**
42. What is a target? **Page # 66**
43. How is a target introduced? **Page # 67**
46. What are receptive & expressive processing drills? **Page # 71**

What sensory issues affect autistic & PDD children?

QUESTION 16

Everyone encounters unpleasant or distracting sensory experiences. Fingernails scratching against a chalkboard, an itchy sweater or a very bright light are common sensory issues. Sensory issues can be uncomfortable and distracting and they often depend on the individual. It is difficult for some people to take an exam while music is playing. Others concentrate very well with music playing in the background. One person may cringe at the sound of squeaky brakes and another may not even notice the sound. Some people enjoy very light touches on their skin and some people find the sensation irritating.

Sensory issues are very prevalent in autism cases. An autistic child may not be able to filter out sounds or tolerate hugs, while another autistic child may be oblivious to sounds and crave hugs. It is common for an autistic child to have no reaction to a loud bang. For this reason, many autistic children are thought to have hearing problems. Conversely, it is also common for an autistic child to have exaggerated responses to sound. A child with sensory issues has difficulty filtering sensory input. The child's system does not know what to block out and what to receive.

All of the senses are involved in sensory issues. Basically, the child's sense is either hypersensitive or hyposensitive. If the sense is hypersensitive, the child is overloaded with sensation. The child will seek to block out sensory input. If the sense is hyposensitive, the child will seek stimulation. For example, a child whose sense of hearing is hyperactive may hum and cover his ears. A child with a hyposensitive sense of hearing may raise and lower the volume on the radio.

Sensory issues can affect a child's ability to pay attention. The child may exhibit negative behaviors or frequently tantrum. It is sometimes difficult to tell whether a behavior is the result of a sensory issue, but there are steps that the treatment team takes to recognize and address sensory issues. Sensory integration activities are used to help the child organize sensory input by addressing sensory systems.

Now, you might be wondering ....

17. What are tactile, vestibular and proprioceptive systems? **Page # 28**
18. How do self-stimulatory behaviors involve the senses? **Page # 29**
19. What is perseveration? **Page # 31**
20. What is echolalia? **Page # 32**
21. How does an autistic child use echolalia to communicate? **Page # 34**
62. How is 'desensitizing,' used in therapy with sensory issues? **Page #99**
77. What are some strategies to help an autistic child integrate sensory information? **Page # 121**

QUESTION 17

What are tactile, vestibular and proprioceptive systems?

Some children with pervasive developmental disorders, such as autism, may have dysfunctional sensory systems, making it difficult for the child to process information taken in through the senses. When working with a client, the therapist engages him in activities that involve three primary senses: tactile, vestibular and proprioceptive.

The tactile sensory system is touch. The child needs to be able to interpret sensations caused by his environment, helping the child to navigate through his environment safely. When there is a disorder in the tactile sense, the child may not perceive his environment correctly. There are numerous safety concerns with a child who has tactile difficulties because the child may not process pain. He may continue to hold onto a hot plate even though it is burning him or not respond to puncture wounds.

The vestibular system helps the child detect movement. This sense can be either hyperactive or hypoactive. If the vestibular sensory system is hyperactive, the child will avoid activities that involve movement. If the vestibular system is hypoactive, the child will seek out activities that involve movement.

The proprioceptive sensory system controls the child's ability to automatically adjust his body to different situations. Working on a sub-conscious level, the child's body automatically adjusts and balances while walking, climbing or even sitting. The proprioceptive sensory system also includes fine motor skills, like coloring or buttoning a shirt. The proprioceptive sensory system also controls motor planning. This is the child's ability to coordinate different motor tasks to complete an activity.

Dysfunction in these three systems manifests a number of ways. A child with disorders in the sensory systems may have difficulty with speech. They may struggle through fine motor activities. They may be clumsy or overactive. Sometimes the senses over-react to input and other times they do not react enough. The therapist uses sensory integration exercises to help the children organize sensory input and in turn help diminish distress caused by sensory issues.

Now, you might be wondering ....

60. What are some activities that help special needs children with fine and gross motor faculties? **Page # 97**
75. What strategies are used to reduce self-stimulatory behaviors? **Page # 118**
77. What are some strategies to help an autistic child integrate sensory information? **Page # 121**
100. I think I want to work with special needs children, where should I start? **Page # 159**

How do self-stimulatory behaviors involve the senses?

Typical self-stimulatory behaviors, such as the repeated movement of body parts, stimulate the senses. Therapists see these behaviors frequently and use their knowledge of them to determine treatment options. Here are some examples:

1. Visual self-stimulatory behaviors involve information received through the eyes.

Hand flapping is a common visual stim. The child simply flaps his hands rapidly in front of his eyes. A child may also flap an object. Blinking repetitively and squinting are also visual stims. A child may look through, then over, his glasses repetitively. Also, the child may line objects in order, then stare at them while rocking back-and-forth.

2. Auditory self-stimulatory behaviors involve information received through the ears.

A child may make vocal sounds repetitively. The child may cover his ears and release them repeatedly while continuing a constant hum. A child may also tap his ears or tap objects together close to his ears.

3. Tactile self-stimulatory behaviors involve information received through touch.

Scratching is a common tactile stim. The child may scratch his skin repeatedly or he may rhythmically scratch a surface. The child may run his hands under his clothes. Playing with hair or rubbing materials between fingers relate to tactile stimulatory behavior.

4. Gustatory self-stimulatory behaviors involve information received through taste.

The child may mouth objects, suck on his fingers and chew on his hair. Some children lick objects repeatedly. For example, a child may lick a television screen or a computer screen.

5. Olfactory self-stimulatory behaviors are tied to gustatory behaviors. They involve information received through smell.

Sniffing is a less common self-stimulatory behavior. The child may sniff objects repeatedly. The child may smell another person, especially if the person is wearing cologne or perfume.

Other systems - Self-stimulatory behaviors are linked to the vestibular and proprioceptive systems. Information received by the vestibule located in the inner ear is linked to the vestibular system. This system helps the individual detect motion. Self-stimulatory behaviors associated with the vestibular system include rocking and spinning.

The proprioceptive system involves information about the relative positions of parts of the body. This system works on a subconscious level, based upon sensations located in muscles, ligaments and joints. Self-stimulatory behaviors associated with the proprioceptive system include wrapping arms inside a shirt and burrowing into cushions.

Self-stimulatory behaviors are difficult to eliminate and are often replaced by other behaviors. A therapist works to help the child control self-stimulatory behaviors that distract him from important tasks or in some way disrupt the child's environment.

Now, you might be wondering ....

16. What sensory issues affect autistic & PDD children? **Page # 27**
17. What are tactile, vestibular and proprioceptive systems? **Page # 28**
25. What deficiencies do autistic children have with auditory processing? **Page # 38**
38. What is a drill? **Page # 58**
39. How do drills adhere to the treatment plan? **Page # 60**
40. How do drills relate to applied behavioral analysis? **Page # 62**
49. What is the treatment plan? **Page # 76**
61. What are some examples of engaging activities? **Page # 98**
62. How is 'desensitizing,' used in therapy with sensory issues? **Page # 99**
75. What strategies are used to reduce self-stimulatory behaviors? **Page # 118**
77. What are some strategies to help an autistic child integrate sensory information? **Page # 121**

What is perseveration and how does it relate to self-stimulatory behaviors?

QUESTION 19

Perseveration is the repetition of actions or statements. Almost all children perseverate a little. Many children love to hear the same song over and over. Some ask to have the same story repeated and some love to watch a favorite movie again and again. Some children ask, "Are we there yet?" several times during a long trip. Children diagnosed within the autism spectrum of disorders take perseveration to the extreme.

A child with PDD may rewind a movie to one particular scene or rewind a song so the singer repeats the same word over and over again. Some children like to press the same button on electronic toys repeatedly. I worked with a child who pressed the same button on a toy so often that he wore a divot into it. Another child had figured out a pattern in her interactive toy and was able to press the correct response before the toy could ask the question. This way, she could hear, "You did great!" over and over.

Perseveration may also include repetition of body movements, as seen in many self-stimulatory behaviors like hand flapping. A child may also like to place objects in a line. The child may also stack toys in a particular order. With these behaviors, the therapist addresses the problem by simply disrupting the order. He can do this by picking the objects up or knocking them out of sequence and prompting the child to put them away.

Addressing perseveration in actions is a little different than addressing the problem with language. It is ironic that we work so hard to encourage a child to use language, then we work so hard to encourage the child to use less language. We have to consider how the language functions. When a child uses language to perseverate, he may repeat the same statement or ask the same question over and over again. This is not functional communication, making it necessary to address it as a part of therapy.

Now, you might be wondering ....

25. What deficiencies do autistic children have with auditory processing? **Page # 38**
26. What are executive function deficits? **Page # 39**
27. How do autistic and PDD children process language? **Page # 40**
28. What is applied behavioral analysis? **Page # 42**
29. What is behavior? **Page # 44**
76. What strategies are used to reduce verbal perseveration? **Page # 119**
89. What books are available to help me learn more about working with special needs children? **Page # 143**
100. I think I want to work with special needs children, where should I start? **Page # 159**

QUESTION 20

What is echolalia?

Not all verbal speech is used to communicate. In many cases, the child who uses language does not intend to interact with another person. An autistic child may be very vocal and still have significant communication problems. In order for language to be considered communication, it must serve some social purpose.

Echolalia is a verbal behavior in which the child mimics what he hears repeatedly. The child may repeat one word, a sentence or a whole chunk of dialogue. The child may use the same vocal tones and inflection as the original speaker. The child does this immediately following the original utterance or may repeat utterances he heard weeks or even years ago.

Echolalia is part of normal language development. Young children often repeat what they hear. It is part of the learning process. The autistic child who uses echolalia does this longer than a normal child and the autistic child uses echolalia more frequently. As children develop spontaneous language, the instances of echolalia diminish. This is true for normally developing children as well as autistic children.

In some cases, echolalia does not serve a communicative purpose. Children use echolalia in different ways. Many verbal children diagnosed within the autism spectrum of disorders engage in T.V. talk. The child who uses T.V. talk memorizes chunks of dialogue from videos or television shows and repeats the dialogue repeatedly. Whether the child is using utterances heard on television or during everyday interactions, the child uses language without expecting a response from another person. The utterance does not seem to fit into the context of events. This does not mean that the utterance has no purpose at all. The following are some common situations surrounding echolalia:

1. The child may engage in the behavior when he is in a stressful situation.

Repeating memorized chunks of language may be used as a self-stimulatory behavior. The repetition is often comforting and the stim helps the child to calm himself. For example, a child who is nervous during a visit to the doctor's office may repeat statements his doctor made during the last visit.

2. The utterances may be triggered by environment.

A child may say, "Everyone wait for their turn," while approaching an occupied swing at the park. The utterance helps the child to wait but it is not intended to communicate anything to another individual.

3. The child may use echolalia to follow steps in a task.

A child who is making a sandwich may say, "Get the bread. Open the refrigerator. Don't hold the jar by the lid…" The child is giving himself the same directions he previously heard during the same task.

In these examples, the echolalia serves a purpose, but the purpose is not social communication. In some cases, echolalia is used to communicate. How this occurs is valuable information for gaining understanding of the child's methods for processing information. A therapist will watch and record much of this to help other team members determine the appropriate course for treatment.

Now, you might be wondering ….

21. How does an autistic child use echolalia to communicate? **Page # 34**
23. What is functional language? **Page # 36**
25. What deficiencies do autistic children have with auditory processing? **Page # 38**
27. How do autistic and PDD children process language? **Page # 40**
28. What is applied behavioral analysis? **Page # 42**
49. What is the treatment plan? **Page # 76**
77. What are some strategies to help an autistic child integrate sensory information? **Page # 121**

Some quick facts about Echolalia

Echolalia has been shown to occur in more than 75% of the cases of autism, but is also present in a number of other conditions. For example, people suffering from Tourette's syndrome or even schizophrenia normally have some form of echolalia.

Involuntary echolalia is usually referred to as a *tic*. For autistic cases, echolalia is most often voluntary and serves some purpose. Just as with other behaviors, understanding that purpose is difficult and should only be achieved through the systematic process established and guided by the child's treatment plan.

QUESTION 21
How does an autistic child use echolalia to communicate?

The way a child uses echolalia for communication shows how the child processes information. Sometimes an autistic child processes whole statements without understanding individual words. The child may not know what the individual words in the phrase mean. For example, an autistic child may say, "What a good job!" after he is given a present. The child is using the phrase because he associates it with a pleasant experience. He does not mean to tell anyone they are doing a good job, he means to communicate excitement about the present. In the past, he was rewarded and praised for doing a good job. The reward and praise resulted in a positive emotion. By repeating this phrase, even though it is out of context, he communicates that a similar emotion is being experienced.

Echolalia may also be used for functional communication in the following ways:

1. Making requests - The child uses echolalia to ask for a desired object or activity. The child may say, "Everyone get their snack," to indicate that he would like something to eat.
2. Protesting - The child uses echolalia to communicate dissent. The child may say, "Now appearing on DVD and videocassette," while his parents are watching the news.
3. Agreeing - The child uses echolalia to say, "Yes." The child may repeat, "Do you have to use the restroom?" to communicate that he needs to use the restroom.
4. Initiating communication - The child uses echolalia to initiate interaction with others. The child may walk up to a group of children and say, "It was a cold and rainy night." The statement is related to a program he saw and it is in his thoughts. He uses the phrase to communicate that he notices other people and he is trying to interact with them.
5. Reciprocating conversation - The child uses echolalia when he understands that a response it required during a conversation. The child may respond to the question, "What are you going to do after therapy today?" with, "Check your schedule." The child knows that a response is required and he uses the last word he hears as a link to his statement. He uses a schedule in therapy and makes the statement because the original question includes the word, "therapy."

It is very promising when a child uses echolalia as a form of communication. It illustrates that the child is beginning to acknowledge other people. A therapist needs to pay very close attention to how the child uses echolalia, because it reveals a great deal about their level of ability with regards to communication.

Now, you might be wondering ....
20. What is echolalia? **Page # 32**
23. What is functional language? **Page # 36**
27. How do autistic and PDD children process language? **Page # 40**

What is theory of mind?

QUESTION 22

Theory of mind is a relatively new concept that emerged in the early to middle 1990's. The theory explores the notion that autistic individuals do not understand that other people have different thoughts than they do. An autistic child can not see things from another person's point of view and is unable to interpret another person's feelings. They have difficulty understanding that other people think differently. For example, if an autistic child is interested in trains, he believes that everyone else is interested in trains.

It's not so much that the autistic child lacks empathy; it's more that the child believes that everyone shares the same thoughts and emotions. This all may stem from the child's lack of body awareness. They may not be able to percieve their body as their own or as being separate from surroundings. In much the same way, theory of mind extends to include the child's own consciousness (much like a lack of body awareness, the child misinterprets his or her own consciousness).

Here is an example of an autistic child that illustrates theory of mind and what it suggests. A child's mother told him to be careful with a toy. She told him that the toy is from his grandmother and she will be sad if he breaks it. After his mother makes the statement, the child began to ask, "Where's grandma?" He began repeating, "Grandma's sad." He whined and acted as if he was crying. The child seemed to equate his grandmother's being sad to his being sad. The child was distracted by the emotion and continued to act sad throughout the first part of his therapy. The therapist drew a happy face and said, "Grandma is happy." The child repeated, "Grandma's happy," and continued working without whining. In this case, the child does not lack empathy, **he lacks the understanding that one person can be sad while another is happy.** Telling the child that grandma is sad is like telling him that he is sad.

Although the autistic child has difficulty discerning his thoughts and feelings from thoughts and feelings of other people, he still appears to lack empathy. This lack of empathy does not stem from uncaring, but from misunderstanding and the inability to interpret social cues. Therapists use a number of techniques to help autistic children learn how to better interpret the wants and needs of others. Social stories are one such tool.

Now, you might be wondering ....

15. What is body awareness? **Page # 26**
16. What sensory issues affect autistic & PDD children? **Page # 27**
28. What is applied behavioral analysis? **Page # 42**
64. How are social stories used in shaping? **Page # 102**
65. What does a typical social story look like? **Page # 104**

QUESTION 23

What is functional language?

Functional language is language that serves a purpose. It is a common component in a child's therapy if improved communication skills are a goal in the treatment plan. The cause and effect cycle of Applied Behavioral Analysis and discrete trial drills prepares the child to recognize that an action facilitates a consequence. Teaching functional language helps the child recognize that words can facilitate consequences. This leads the child to communicate and socialize with others.

An example of a word that children almost always use functionally is, "More." A child being pushed on the swing uses the word, "more," to continue the activity. Nonverbal children would use the sign for, "more," in the same situation. This functional word is useful because it yields a concrete consequence. A preferred play item or activity are powerful motivators when introducing and maintaining a child's use of functional language. "More," is one of the most common functional words found in a child's program book.

Another word that is commonly found in a program book is, "Help." This functional word is useful because, through it, the child learns a way to connect with others and lessen frustration. "Help," takes a little more time and effort to teach, but once the child understands the result of using the word, it usually becomes very easy to maintain.

Autistic children acquire language intellectually, not incidentally, so before language can be used functionally, it has to be *learned*. An autisitic child would learn simple language the way that you would learn concepts in a Biology or Calculus class. Applied Behavior Analysis breaks this task into small steps. To teach the child functional language it often helps to begin with NVI (non-verbal imitation) or work with the word after the sign has been mastered in sign language drills. After this, the therapist works with the child's understanding of language by moving outside of the drills and using the language in more general settings.

Now, you might be wondering ....

27. How do autistic and PDD children process language? **Page # 40**
28. What is applied behavioral analysis? **Page # 42**
38. What is a drill? **Page # 58**
39. How do drills adhere to the treatment plan? **Page # 60**
40. How do drills relate to applied behavioral analysis? **Page # 62**

What is non-verbal imitation?

QUESTION 24

NVI is non-verbal imitation. Nonverbal imitation is another visual drill found early on in a child's behavioral program. Wiht NVI, a therapist uses the Discrete Stimulus, "Do this," and performs a simple one-step action. If the child does not imitate, the therapist uses a hand-over-hand (physical) prompt to help the child process the command.

Imitation is difficult for children with autism. Imitation requires the child to pay attention to the therapist and their actions. The child will often be able to do the action independently, but needs to actually learn the process of imitating. At times, *mass prompting* is used. Mass prompting in nonverbal imitation is simply using the same physical prompt repeatedly until the child makes the motion independently. Imitation is valuable because it can be used to learn new skills. The obstacle is getting the child to understand what is expected.

Using objects in nonverbal imitation helps catch the child's attention and may motivate them to imitate naturally. For example, objects that make noises and are visually interesting can help drive therapy forward. A rattle is a prime example of a good object to use in nonverbal imitation drills. The child may not intend to imitate, but is motivated by the noise to repeat an action. This is a great teaching opportunity. Rewarding the child immediately after the they use the rattle to make a noise reinforces imitation.

Nonverbal imitation with objects can easily extend to everyday objects like a toothbrush or a spoon. Encouraging the child's family to use the same objects used in therapy will help the child develop and maintain the skill. Nonverbal imitation drills may not use objects at all. Clapping is a common nonverbal imitation target found in many program books. Clapping is a good choice because the child can see his hands in the drill. If you direct a child to touch his nose, he will not be able to see the action completely. Also, many autistic children have difficulty with body awareness and may not be able to follow through without seeing the activity. NVI is just one step on the long path to teaching a child how to use functional language, a step on their way to functioning more successfully in social situations.

Now, you might be wondering ....

23. What is functional language? **Page # 36**
36. What are discrete trials? **Page # 54**
39. How do drills adhere to the treatment plan? **Page # 60**
40. How do drills relate to applied behavioral analysis? **Page # 62**
41. What is a discrete stimulus or SD? **Page # 64**

QUESTION 25

What deficiencies do autistic children have with auditory processing?

People diagnosed within the autism spectrum of disorders often have great difficulty interpreting sounds. One significant problem when addressing auditory processing is teaching a client that a sound represents something. This is very difficult for most autistic children to understand. This is why a child's treatment plan usually prescribes the use of visual communication tools, such as sign language and a Picture Exchange Communication System (PECS), to help the client to begin to understand sounds.

Auditory sounds are not tangible. They are invisible and transitory. A sentence can seem like one connected unit of sound to an autistic person. Adding visuals helps the child process auditory sounds, especially if the child is consistently presented visuals with spoken words. This is especially important when using action words. Making motions that represent the desired action shows the child what is expected. This understanding, in turn, reduces frustration, leading to fewer tantrums.

We often take our ability to process spoken words for granted and it is easy to confuse someone who has difficulty with auditory processing. For example, I worked with a girl who mastered the word, "wait," and she was ready to move on to the next target on the drill's target sheet. She had great difficulty with the following word, "want." She became agitated when we worked on the drill. It took a few sessions before I noticed the similarity between the two words. We were also working on the number one (want - wait - one) in another drill. That also added to the child's frustration.

Therapists have to keep the sounds of words in mind. Autistic children have difficulty discriminating between "five" and "nine" in numbers and "B" and "D" in letters. Grouping these similar-sounding targets together early may lead to frustration, which slows progress. The word, "right," is another example of a confusing word. Do we mean correct? Are we referring to a direction? The English language is very complex and its complexities are compounded as the child progresses, especially when the language involves social components. We commonly use idioms and figurative language, both of which are extremely difficult for an autistic person to understand.

Now, you might be wondering ....

16. What sensory issues affect autistic & PDD children? **Page # 27**
28. What is applied behavioral analysis? **Page # 42**
58. What is PECS? **Page # 93**
73. What strategies are used for teaching idioms? **Page # 115**

What are executive function deficits?

QUESTION 26

Executive function deficit is an umbrella term used when a child has a problem with one or several cognitive processes. These cognitive processes are advanced. They are rarely discussed directly in therapy or in the treatment plan. However, it is helpful to be familiar with these in order to be aware of how some programs are designed to work with the child's abilities and strengths.

There are five cognitive processes:
1. **Working memory** - Working memory is a process that enables the child to keep one thought in mind while updating it with new information. We use working memory when completing steps in a task.
2. **Cognitive flexibility** - Cognitive flexibility requires the child to toggle between ideas. The process helps the child relate new information to a concept and adapt his thinking to the new information. We use cognitive flexibility when we brainstorm different ideas or options.
3. **Organizing and planning** - Organizing and planning require the child to be able to think ahead and prepare for upcoming events. We use organizing and planning processes when we get ready for work or school.
4. **Problem solving** - Problem solving skills require the child to be able to develop solutions to problems. We use problem solving skills when we arrive at ways to complete tasks.
5. **Cognitive inhibition** - Cognitive inhibition requires the child to be able to restrain himself from responding until he has thought the task through. We use cognitive inhibition when we wait to listen to the next direction before taking the next step.

These five processes often work together. For example, we use working memory while using problem-solving skills. Problem-solving skills may also require cognitive flexibility. When we solve a problem, we have to keep the original problem in mind (using working memory) while coming up with various ways of solving the problem (using cognitive flexibility). Most of us simply complete tasks or organize activities without considering the cognitive processes involved. When working with children with executive functioning deficits, it helps to break the task down according to the cognitive processes used. A therapist can engage a child in a number of activities that help the child develop these cognitive processes.

Now, you might be wondering ....

28. What is applied behavioral analysis? **Page # 42**
71. What strategies are used to engage autistic children in activities? **Page # 111**
100. I think I want to work with special needs children, where should I start? **Page # 159**

QUESTION 27
How do autistic and PDD children process language?

Young children acquire language as they communicate during everyday activities. An autistic child has to learn language intellectually. Language does not come naturally nor is it effortlessly attained. Communication on all levels is difficult for an autistic person. Even facial expressions are arduous for an autistic person to interpret. Poetic elements found in common speech are challenging for many children and even more so for an autistic child.

The main problem with figurative language, for someone who is autistic, is that they tend to take such language literally. This is common during early development. I remember my mother used to say, "Watch your eyes," before turning on a light in a dark room. I did not understand what she expected me to do. It was impossible for me to watch my own eyes without looking in a mirror.

I worked with a boy who was in first grade in a regular classroom. He would become very agitated when the teacher would say, "Eyes on me." His agitation was heightened when the teacher would make a, '*V*,' with her index and middle finger and point them at his eyes, then turning them towards her while saying, "Eyes on me." He thought that she literally wanted him to put his eyes on her.

Idioms and figurative language are strange and puzzling for many autistic children. A child who struggles with communication on a daily basis is easily exasperated when language does not take on the meaning the child has learned. Sarcasm should also be avoided because it is confusing. If the child throws the crayons on the floor and the therapist says, "That's just great," the child will probably take the literal meaning of the statement to be true.

Working in this field, you get a sense for how clients process and understand language. You use this understanding to alter activities and drills in a way that helps the child to develop their communication skills, but these alterations take place within the established system for therapy and under the guidance of the treatment team as a whole.

Now, you might be wondering ....

22. What is theory of mind? **Page # 35**
23. What is functional language? **Page # 36**
25. What deficiencies do autistic children have with auditory processing? **Page # 38**
28. What is applied behavioral analysis? **Page # 42**
49. What is the treatment plan? **Page # 76**
94. What are some methods for autism treatment aside from ABA? **Page # 150**

Your Questions Answered on...

**THERAPY IN ACTION
BASICS, TERMS & PHASES**

28. What is applied behavioral analysis? **Page # 42**
29. What is behavior? **Page # 44**
30. What are the functions of behavior? **Page # 46**
31. What are the antecedents to behavior? **Page # 48**
32. What are consequences for behavior? **Page # 50**
33. What are non-negotiable behaviors? **Page # 51**
34. What is Behaviorism? **Page # 52**
35. How are positive and negative reinforcement used in therapy? **Page # 53**
36. What are discrete trials? **Page # 54**
37. What are the phases of discrete trial drills? **Page # 56**
38. What is a drill? **Page # 58**
39. How do drills adhere to the treatment plan? **Page # 60**
40. How do drills relate to applied behavioral analysis? **Page # 62**
41. What is a discrete stimulus or SD? **Page # 64**
42. What is a target? **Page # 66**
43. How is a target introduced? **Page # 67**
44. What if a child can not master a target? **Page # 68**
45. What is random rotation? **Page # 69**
46. What are receptive & expressive processing drills? **Page # 71**
47. What is the difference between sign language and receptive processing drills? **Page # 72**
48. How does a therapist use sign language in drills? **Page # 73**

QUESTION 28: What is Applied Behavioral Analysis?

Applied Behavioral Analysis is a comprehensive program or, "intervention," that has yielded notable results in the treatment of autism. ABA has roots in the behaviorist splinter of Psychology. The approach focuses on rewarding positive behavior and discounting negative behavior.

ABA breaks a task down into small steps. As the child masters each step another one is introduced. This approach is effective for individuals who have difficulty staying focused, driving progress forward by motivating through the use of positive and negative reinforcement.

Applied Behavior Analysis is a practice that leads to the acquisition of new skills. This practice not only focuses on learning, but on maintaining and using acquired skills in all settings. Normally, very young children acquire language and social skills naturally through experiencing everyday activities. The autistic population has to acquire language and social skills intellectually, the way most children learn how to read or add. Using methods dictated through ABA helps a therapist to teach special children these skills.

Elements of ABA include:

1. **Application.** The skills acquired through ABA should have some social significance and should be applicable to everyday environments and situations.
2. **Behavioral.** The goals in the treatment plan are related to behaviors.
3. **Analytic.** The data should prove that a change in the child's behavior results from the therapy.
4. **Methodical.** The techniques that one uses should be described in enough detail that another therapist can duplicate them without direct supervision.
5. **Systematic.** There should be relevance to established behavioral approaches.
6. **Effective.** The changes in the child's behavior should be significant.
7. **Generality.** The change in behavior should been seen in a variety of settings and situations.

The elements of Applied Behavior Analysis reflect organization and consistency. Autistic children do not acquire much information from the environment unless the environment is structured. This system helps create a very structured environment that is conducive to learning. A big part of the structured environment is a reward system. Using rewards to shape behavior is a powerful and defining tool in ABA.

Discrete trial teaching is a common method used in Applied Behavior Analysis. Discrete trials involve drills where the therapist gives a command (SD or stimulus) that is usually accompanied by a target. The goal is for the client to engage in the correct response for the stimulus. The target is there to receive the action. For example a therapist may give the SD, "touch," and then the target, "nose." If the client touches their nose, they are rewarded. If they do not, more work needs to be done.

ABA involves more that discrete trial training. Applied Behavior Analysis is practiced in various settings and in everyday situations. A therapist begins teaching skills in discrete trial, but practices those mastered skills in general settings. The new skills also need to be practiced with family members in the child's natural environment.

Now, you might be wondering ....

29. What is behavior? **Page # 44**
35. How are positive and negative reinforcement used in therapy? **Page # 53**
36. What are discrete trials? **Page # 54**
37. What are the phases of discrete trial drills? **Page # 56**
38. What is a drill? **Page # 58**
40. How do drills relate to applied behavioral analysis? **Page # 62**
94. What are some methods for autism treatment aside from ABA? **Page # 150**

The ABA debate

Though Applied Behavioral Analysis is the foundation on which Wraparound programs are designed, not all professionals who work with special needs children agree with its methods. Programs such as the Son-Rise and others use methods and a belief system that are different from what ABA dictates.

Before you begin your career, be certain to pay attention to these methodologies and the history behind them (most of this you can find in this guide). If working with special needs children is what you really want to do, it's best to work within a program that fits your own beliefs and doesn't require you to act against your own nature. This quick and easy kind of research can go a long way towards helping you find that specific position that really compliments who you are.

QUESTION 29

What is behavior?

This seems like an odd and obvious question, but behavior is more complicated than it seems. Many behaviorists consider behavior to be a form of communication. Nearly every action has a purpose. In my career, I have actually seen blinking listed as a behavior in a treatment program. Since blinking can be varied and controlled, it can be used as communication and it can be a behavior, whether intentional or not. It is important to remember that many of the behaviors we address when working with autistic children are like blinking to them. They're not entirely aware of either the behavior or what it is intended to communicate.

Behavior & ABA - The main goal of Applied Behavioral Analysis is to target specific behaviors and shape them systematically. Applied Behavior Analysis is a product of a scientific approach to psychology known as Behaviorism. The approach is clinical and objective, so behavior in ABA has to be observable and measurable. It is easy to confuse inner workings with behavior. For example, a therapist may write that a child, during a therapeutic session, "became angry," when instructed to sit at his workstation. Anger is not a measurable, objective, behavior. This puts it outside of the therapist's scope. Instead of recording the action as, 'anger,' the therapist should write that the child screamed and threw himself on the floor when instructed to sit at the workstation. The behavior, and specific actions, not the emotions, are the focus for the professional.

Objective Treatment - Without a focus on specific, measurable, behaviors, there would be no systematic basis for a treatment plan. The therapist can take data on the frequency and duration of behaviors. For example, in the case of a tantrum a therapist would record that the child screamed and threw himself on the floor *three times* during a *fifteen-minute span of time*. Each incident lasted *thirty seconds*. This helps the behavior specialist develop goals in the treatment plan. In this example, if those behaviors prevail during transitions between activities, the behavior specialist could target making smooth transitions as a goal. The smooth transitions will not happen overnight, so a short-term goal would be that the child transitions without a tantrum between four activities in a thirty minute period.

A therapist works toward the short-term goal in steps by using interventions outlined in the treatment plan. In the transition example, interventions may include using a visual schedule of activities. The child can help the therapist create a schedule, designing a session that alternates between work and play activities. The therapist, in this type of schedule, would use primary reinforcement or praise to motivate the child to transition and this motivation would in turn reduce the frequency of tantrums.

The interventions depend on the child's needs and strengths. It is much easier to decide how to intervene on behavior than to decide how to intervene on emotions. The child's emotions are not within the therapist's control. A behavior specialist would not create a goal around an emotion. For example, a goal such as, "The child will transition without becoming angry three times over a thirty-minute period," is not measurable. However, making the goal read, "The child will transition without making loud noises or laying on the floor three times over a thirty minute period," is measurable. A therapist is able to work with this goal because it is objective.

Now, you might be wondering ....

30. What are the functions of behavior? **Page # 46**
31. What are the antecedents to behavior? **Page # 48**
32. What are consequences for behavior? **Page # 50**
33. What are non-negotiable behaviors? **Page # 51**
35. How are positive and negative reinforcement used in therapy? **Page # 53**
36. What are discrete trials? **Page # 54**
37. What are the phases of discrete trial drills? **Page # 56**
63. How does a therapist, 'shape,' behavior? **Page # 100**
100. I think I want to work with special needs children, where should I start? **Page # 159**

Am I going to use this?

It's interesting how rarely, in the day-to-day workplace, that the foundations for a professional field are discussed. Still, it's always important to have a firm grasp of these foundations and constantly work to improve your understanding of them. The simple question of - What is behavior? - can seem like a minor issue. We all know what behavior is, don't we?

As a therapist in an ABA based program, my impressions of something as simple as, 'behavior,' have been constantly tested, changed, re-tested and redefined. I think this is what makes working with special needs children such an excellent field for students of behavior, learning and psychology.

QUESTION 30: What are the functions of behavior?

A therapist will not be concerned with any particular emotion behind a child's behavior. However, they are concerned with the functions of the child's behavior. A child who screams and throws himself on the floor may be angry. He could be frustrated. These issues are not the focus of therapy. The main goal of the therapist is to help the child navigate through everyday situations without behavior problems. In order to address the behavior, it is helpful to articulate the function of the behavior in terms relative to these situations.

There are six functions of behavior:

1. Attention:

Some behaviors are used to gain attention. The child behaves a certain way to get attention from others around him. For example, the child may throw a toy and look to his mother for her response.

2. Wants:

The child may use a behavior to get an object of desire or to engage in a preferred activity. For example, the child may cry and reach for a toy in a store.

3. Avoidance:

The child may use a behavior to avoid a task. For example, the child may have a tantrum to avoid going onto the school bus.

4. Self-stimulatory:

Some behaviors address sensory needs. The child uses the behavior to meet a stimulatory need. For example, the child flips through pages in a book repeatedly to stimulate tactile senses.

5. Physical:

Some behaviors address physical needs. For example, the child may cry easily or put his head on the table if he is tired.

6. Task completion:

The child uses behavior to finish a task. He may throw a piece of a puzzle on the floor if he can't fit it into the puzzle.

Determining the function of a behavior is not always easy and it does take time. The child's treatment team works together to determine how a behavior functions. This is never achieved through assumptions. I once left a shift early because I was convinced that the child was tired. She laid down on the floor. She was lethargic and slow in her actions. She cried each time I even spoke to her and she turned her head from me. During her break, she went to her bed and acted like she was sleeping. Of course, I ended the shift early and left. The next day, her mother told me that the girl had gotten out of bed once my car left their driveway. She was awake and alert after I left. The function of the behavior was not to meet the physical need for sleep. The function of the behavior was avoidance. The child wanted to avoid working.

In order to really determine the function of a consistent behavior, the child's team must record the antecedent to the behavior, as well as the consequences for the behavior. With this data, the behaviorist, case manager and therapist begin to unlock the riddle of the child's behavior and set attainable goals to move the therapy forward.

Now, you might be wondering ....

9. What treatment program is used most frequently? **Page # 16**
31. What are the antecedents to behavior? **Page # 48**
32. What are consequences for behavior? **Page # 50**
33. What are non-negotiable behaviors? **Page # 51**
35. How are positive and negative reinforcement used in therapy? **Page # 53**
36. What are discrete trials? **Page # 54**
37. What are the phases of discrete trial drills? **Page # 56**
63. How does a therapist, 'shape,' behavior? **Page # 100**
72. What are some strategies for teaching replacement behaviors? **Page # 113**
74. What strategies are used to motivate autistic children? **Page # 117**
75. What strategies are used to reduce self-stimulatory behaviors? **Page # 118**
93. What are some important moments in applied behavioral analysis? **Page # 148**
94. What are some methods for autism treatment aside from ABA? **Page # 150**
95. Where are some websites where I can learn more about Wraparound? **Page # 152**
96. What are some different roles that I can take in a career spent working with special needs children? **Page # 153**

QUESTION 31

What are the antecedents to behavior?

The antecedent to a behavior is what occurs immediately before the behavior. The therapist takes data on what occurred immediately prior to the behavior. An antecedent is not always easy to recognize even when data is collected on a daily basis. Sometimes it takes an outside observer to see what is really happening in order to establish the antecedent.

I took data on a behavior that occurred on a daily basis with one of my clients. Each time I prompted the child to come to the workstation, the child had a tantrum. I recorded the duration and frequency of the behavior and I made a note that the antecedent was me saying, "Come sit." However, when the behavior specialist observed one of the shifts, she noticed that the antecedent was not actually the command to come sit at the workstation. The behavior specialist noticed that I would give the command, "Come sit," then I would say something else, such as, "Good job," while the child approached the workstation. It turned out that the antecedent to the child's behavior was not the command to sit, it was the utterances I made as the child was following the direction.

The tantrums stopped once I refrained from making statements as the child came to the workstation. The child may have been confused by the utterances. She may have thought that I was making a second command. She could have been frustrated or angry because she thought that I was saying something else. What she was feeling was not the issue. The behavior was. Once we were able to establish the antecedent to the behavior, we could address the problem. In this case, the child required ample time to follow through with the command before hearing another utterance.

An antecedent can be a number of things. In the example above, the antecedent was extra words for the child to process while following a command. The antecedent can be a time of day. I worked with a child who threw objects at 3:30pm everyday. It took awhile before we noticed that it was the time of day that was the antecedent. We tried different activities, such as playtime, sensory integration and drills and found that the only pattern was the time of day. A particular activity can be an antecedent. The trigger for the behavior may be shapes or letters. The antecedent may be the child's medication. The child could outgrow his dosage or be introduced to a new medicine. The child could be on a new diet. He may not have slept well the night before.

Any number of things can trigger negative behavior. Therapists are mostly concerned with consistently negative behavior. A consistent behavior may happen only on Wednesdays or once each month. This is why it is important to keep detailed data on the child's behavior on a daily basis.

Finding the antecedent to a behavior helps the behavior specialist develop interventions and goals. It also helps the team determine the function of a behavior. In order to determine the function of the behavior, the team has to consider the consequences for the behavior as well.

Now, you might be wondering ....

9. What treatment program is used most frequently? **Page # 16**
30. What are the functions of behavior? **Page # 46**
32. What are consequences for behavior? **Page # 50**
33. What are non-negotiable behaviors? **Page # 51**
35. How are positive and negative reinforcement used in therapy? **Page # 53**
36. What are discrete trials? **Page # 54**
37. What are the phases of discrete trial drills? **Page # 56**
63. How does a therapist, 'shape,' behavior? **Page # 100**
72. What are some strategies for teaching replacement behaviors? **Page # 113**
73. What strategies are used for teaching idioms? **Page # 115**
74. What strategies are used to motivate autistic children? **Page # 117**
75. What strategies are used to reduce self-stimulatory behaviors? **Page # 118**
76. What strategies are used to reduce verbal perseveration? **Page # 119**
93. What are some important moments in Applied Behavioral Analysis? **Page # 148**
94. What are some methods for autism treatment aside from ABA? **Page # 150**
95. Where are some websites where I can learn more about Wraparound? **Page # 152**
96. What are some different roles that I can take in a career spent working with special needs children? **Page # 153**

Journals on Behavior

There are a number of journals that publish articles on behavior as it relates to autistic children. It is good for your career to subscribe to a few journals and keep up with current developments:

1. Journal of Child Psychology and Psychiatry
   (www.blackwellpublishing.com)
2. Journal of Autism and Developmental Disorders
   (www.springer.com)
3. Journal of Child & Adolescent Psychiatry
   (www.jaacap.com)

QUESTION 32
What are the consequences for behavior?

Therapists record consequences for the child's behaviors on a daily basis. The consequence for a behavior is what happens immediately following the behavior. Although the phrase, "consequences for your actions," has negative connotations, a consequence for a behavior may be positive. Each time a child is given positive reinforcement for giving an appropriate response during a drill in therapy, he receives a consequence. Like the antecedent, the consequence is also difficult to ascertain on a single observation.

I had a client that would run to a corner of the room when I would direct him to come to the workstation. I ignored the behavior and redirected him to the task by coming over to the corner and saying, "I do." He would repeat the phrase, reach for my hand and then sit at the table. The behavior specialist noticed that this cycle happened each time I directed him to come to the table. We determined that the consequence for his behavior was my coming over and using the phrase for him to repeat.

Since the cycle happened several times during the shift, we determined that the child was using the sequence of events as a self-stimulatory behavior. It became a ritual that proceeded as follows:

1. Therapist gives command
2. Child runs to corner
3. Therapist says phrase to get child's attention
4. Child repeats phrase and reaches for Therapist's hand
5. Therapist takes his hand and leads him to the workstation

The consequence was actually a chain of events that gave the child stimulatory feedback. He simply wanted to repeat the sequence over and over again. The team found that changing the consequence extinguished the behavior. Instead of following him to the corner I simply said, "nope," and prompted him to come to the work station. This broke the pattern of behavior that he found rewarding.

Consequences help a treatment team determine the function of a behavior. The child may exhibit certain behaviors in order to achieve a certain result. Just like positive reinforcement strengthens a behavior, consequences can strengthen a behavior. A child who stomps his feet and screams while holding onto a toy probably wants to keep the toy. A child who has a tantrum at 5:00pm every evening may want to eat. Determining the consequence helps the team to shape the behavior. The behavior specialist may design an ABC chart for data collection on the child's behavior to help gather data to make these determinations.

What are non-negotiable behaviors?

QUESTION 33

Some behaviors simply should not be ignored. They include any behavior that can lead to damaged property, injury to the child or injury to others. The behavior specialist includes interventions that a therapist uses in case the behavior is non-negotiable. The staff has to be consistent with the family about the consequences for non-negotiable behaviors. Consequences must be clear and immediate.

Some examples of non-negotiable behaviors are:
1. Biting
2. Hitting
3. Throwing objects
4. Kicking
5. Running away
6. Pulling hair

Some self-stimulatory behaviors are non-negotiable. Any behavior that may cause injury to the child is non-negotiable. The non-negotiable self-stimulatory behaviors are commonly self-injurious. The reasons behind self-injurious behaviors are uncertain, but there are a few theories:
1. **The child gets an endorphin rush from the behavior.** The body's natural painkillers are released when the child engages in the self-injurious behavior. These behaviors release chemicals in the brain called beta-endorphins. Beta-endorphins function like opiates.
2. **The child needs release.** He has been over-stimulated and uses the self-injurious behavior to shut everything else out.
3. **The child may have pain in another area of his body.** For example, a child who had a urinary tract infection pulled her hair out of her head. She was unable to communicate that she was in pain, so she used the self-injurious behavior to elevate pain she was feeling elsewhere.
4. **The child may engage in the self-injurious behavior for attention.**
5. **The child may be having difficulty tolerating lights or noises in his environment.**

Now, you might be wondering ....

72. What are some strategies for teaching replacement behaviors? **Page # 113**
75. What strategies are used to reduce self-stimulatory behaviors? **Page # 118**
76. What strategies are used to reduce verbal perseveration? **Page # 119**
77. What are some strategies to help an autistic child integrate sensory information? **Page # 121**

QUESTION 34

What is Behaviorism?

There are a number of ways to carry on a discussion about Behaviorism and how it relates to the work that a therapist or behaviorist does in order to bring treatment to special needs children. For the purpose of this book, we'll consider Behaviorism as it relates to what a therapist does and leave the extensive academic considerations to the classroom.

Behaviorism dictates that behavior should be studied according to observable actions. This branch of Psychology does not discount that organisms think or feel. It simply approaches the study of Psychology with the philosophy that theories should be based on observable evidence. This is a major departure from the introspective methods employed by thinkers such as Sigmund Freud and Carl Jung.

Everything from what a behavioral specialist does when developing a treatment plan, to the actions a therapist takes to put that plan into effect, extend from Behaviorism. For a professional interested in this field, especially one looking to work in an Applied Behavioral Analysis based mental health service, it's very important to understand that treatment for special needs children revolves around observable behavior. When a therapist works with a child, thoughts and feelings take a secondary position to concrete, observable, behavior. Some people entering this field have problems with this aspect of treatment and it is important that you work within a program that agrees with you.

Don't make the mistake of thinking that Applied Behavioral Analysis (the treatment system developed from Behaviorism) expects the therapist to be completely rigid or uncaring. It's just important to understand that with most programs, treatment is considered successful when specific criteria are met. For example, if a therapist is working with a child that has frequent tantrums, the behaviorist will determine exact criteria to meet before this behavior is considered acceptable. The therapist will only be successful when the number of tantrums has been reduced. This will be shown in the data collected during therapeutic sessions. What Behaviorism does not acknowledge are subjective criteria. It's simply not enough for a therapist to believe that a client is, "acting better." There are no, "breakthroughs." The behavior must be recorded and this data needs to show a demonstrated, objective, change.

Now, you might be wondering ....

9. What treatment program is used most frequently? **Page # 16**
28. What is applied behavioral analysis? **Page # 42**
29. What is behavior? **Page # 44**

How are positive and negative reinforcement used in therapy?

Positive and negative reinforcement facilitate compliant behavior through motivation. Each case is unique and each child has different likes and dislikes. It takes a lot of time for a treatment team to find what motivates the client and use it as a tool to shape behavior. Once these are determined, a therapeutic support staff member will begin using primary and secondary motivators during therapy sessions to promote compliant and attentive behavior.

When it comes to creating compliant behavior, the therapist begins with primary reinforcers. These are things such as treats, toys or any physical object that the child values. They are effective for most children and they are very concrete. Primary motivators help the child distinguish between positive and negative consequences by creating a stark contrast. The child gives an appropriate response and is immediately rewarded. These tangible rewards are gradually faded into secondary reinforcers. Secondary motivators include praise, songs or play. Free time is often used as a powerful secondary reinforcer. Eventually, the child will require no reinforcement at all.

Negative reinforcement is not to be confused with punishment. The goal is to strengthen positive behavior and discount negative behavior. Positive and negative reinforcement both strengthen behavior. Punishment and extinction weaken behavior. When using negative reinforcement, a therapist removes an unpleasant element once the desired behavior is reached. Being removed from something unpleasant is rewarding and the behavior that led to the removal will probably be repeated.

The best way to explain the difference between negative reinforcement and punishment is through an example. If a baby's crying stops when you rock him, you will most likely rock the baby again once he cries. The behavior of rocking the baby has been negatively reinforced. On the other hand, if you are punished for a behavior, the behavior is less likely to be repeated. If the baby cries each time that you rock him, the behavior (rocking the baby) has been punished. You probably would not rock the baby again.

This approach is useful when trying to extinguish behaviors like whining. If the client whines while putting a puzzle together, take the puzzle away *once the whining stops*. The child will probably connect the removal of the undesired object (the puzzle) to his ceasing the whining. A therapist may unwittingly use negative reinforcement to increase an undesired behavior. If the therapist takes the puzzle away once the child begins to whine, the therapist has just negatively reinforced the whining. Positive and negative reinforcement both rely heavily on motivation and finding out what motivates the child is the key to a successful behavioral program.

QUESTION 36

What are discrete trials?

Discrete trials are the main component of a teaching strategy used in Applied Behavioral Analysis. It is a method of instruction that uses repetition and cause and effect learning. Discrete trial is a scaffolding method that builds one skill on top of another. Tasks are broken down into small steps and each step is mastered through a series of trials.

Teaching begins with basic skills like sitting at the work station and attending to a task. The directive, "come sit," is often one of the first goals in discrete trial learning. Once the child is able to sit and attend to tasks without tantrums or aggression, he is ready to learn more complex skills, such as social and communication skills. A good example of a fundamental social skill is making eye contact. A newer client will often have, "look at me," as a drill. Sign language and object labeling are fundamental communication skills addressed early in therapy.

There are four elements to discrete trial:

1. The Direction or Question - The therapist initiates a direction or question to the child. It is important to use as few words as possible. An extra word is just one more thing for the child to process. Autistic people often have difficulty processing spoken language. The direction or question should only be one or two words. If the child does not seem to process the direction or question, using gestures can be very helpful.

I worked with a child who demonstrated that she made the association between the word, "cow," and a picture of a cow. The team added *cow* into the child's program. I placed a picture of a cow in front of her and when I gave the direction, "touch cow," the child became confused. I found that if I made a motion modeling touching, and just said, "cow," she followed through appropriately.

2. The Child's Response - Whether correct or incorrect, how the child responds to the stimulus is categorized as the second part to the discrete trial. If the child gives no response at all, it is counted as a, "no response," or incorrect response. If the child gives two incorrect responses, the therapist may prompt the child for the correct response.

A child's response may vary from following through immediately to completely disregarding the direction. It is important to remember that we are shaping behavior and the child's response to the interventions is instrumental in tracking the child's progress. Sometimes the child simply needs a little help to follow directions. A therapist often uses prompts to help the child along.

3. Prompting - A prompt is a clue given to the child to help him give a correct response. A therapist may use a number of techniques to prompt the client. The therapist may point to the correct answer, say the correct answer or even simply look at the correct answer. Some argue that a prompted response should not be rewarded. However, when a task is new to a client, rewarding a prompt helps the client understand what is expected. It also encourages the child to repeat the correct response.

I found that rewarding the child even when he is given a prompt is very effective. One little boy initially turned away once he heard my voice. I directed him to touch the letter 'T' twice. He did not respond. I gave the direction a third time while taking his hand and putting it on the letter. I immediately praised him while giving him a treat. He then faced me and we continued the drill. He learned quickly that there is a positive consequence to his response. Understanding that there are consequences to actions is elemental in shaping behavior.

4. The Consequence for the Response - Correct responses are immediately rewarded and incorrect responses are redirected with a, "nope," or they are ignored or corrected. Therapists use, "nope," instead of, "no." "No," is reserved for more severe infractions. Consequences for responses are either reinforced or discounted. This cause and effect cycle is a very efficient method for producing desired results.

Discrete trial is an important teaching tool. A therapist quickly learns how to use discrete trials effectively to shape the child's behavior. Using Applied Behavior Analysis, you help the child and family practice the skills the child develops in discrete trial in everyday situations. In order to structure a solid learning environment while gaining the child's interest, it is necessary to find what motivates the child and use positive and negative reinforcement.

Now, you might be wondering ....

9. What treatment program is used most frequently? **Page # 16**
28. What is applied behavioral analysis? **Page # 42**
29. What is behavior? **Page # 44**
37. What are the phases of discrete trial drills? **Page # 56**
63. How does a therapist, 'shape,' behavior? **Page # 100**
68. After skills are mastered, how does a therapist generalize these to different settings? **Page # 107**
72. What are some strategies for teaching replacement behaviors? **Page # 113**
73. What strategies are used for teaching idioms? **Page # 115**
74. What strategies are used to motivate autistic children? **Page # 117**
77. What are some strategies to help an autistic child integrate sensory information? **Page # 121**

QUESTION 37

What are the phases of discrete trials?

There are four phases in discrete trial drills:

1. **Matching** - Matching is an action that is usually mastered fairly early in therapy because it is visual in nature. The child is prompted to match two identical items. The items may be numbers, letters, animals, objects or shapes.

An example of a matching drill is Matching Shapes. The therapist gives the child a shape and uses the SD (Discriminitive Stimulus), "match square." The child's targeted response is to match the square to an identical square.

2. **Receptive processing** - After the child becomes familiar with a matching drill and masters a number of targets, the therapist moves the drill into the next phase of receptive processing. In receptive drills, the child demonstrates that he recognizes a target by touching, giving or pointing to it. **This is a little more difficult than matching because the only visual cue is the target itself.** The child has to process the therapist's words and receptively show that he understands.

An example of a receptive drill is **Receptive Shapes**. During this drill, the therapeutic staff support gives the SD, "touch square." The child's targeted response is to touch the square.

3. **Expressive processing** - The therapist moves on to the expressive phase of the drill after the child masters a number of targets in the receptive phase. In expressive drills, the child demonstrates that he recognizes the target by naming it. This is a little more difficult than receptive processing because the child has to process the therapist's words and expressively show that he understands by using language.

An example of an expressive drill is Expressive Shapes. During the drill, the therapist gives the SD, "what shape?" The child's targeted shape is to say, "square." Expressive drills progressively become more complex as the child develops more language. Gradually, the child is prompted to use full sentences and answer social questions. Eventually, the child is also encouraged to use words spontaneously throughout the shift.

The phases of discrete trial drills break down communication and compliance into small steps. Once one step is mastered, the drill moves on to the next phase. Transitioning from one phase to another is sometimes very difficult.

The Big Picture:

Remember, Wraparound is a process and it is not meant to be indefinite. Throughout each phase, there is a team at work. The TSS is the on-site therapist, working with the child through the drills, recording efforts, controlling the environment and handling common problems, such as tantrums or periods of disinterest from the child. The behavior specialist uses the records maintained by the therapist (on Bubble Sheets), to change the child's program and accommodate different needs and abilities. These changes are especially important when transitions are not successful. The case manager manages the treatment, making certain that the therapist has the support needed, the behaviorist is keeping treatment current and making the necessary changes, while also working to coordinate all the other players on the scene (teachers, family, school administrators, etc.).

Now, you might be wondering ....

1. What is a therapist (TSS)? **Page # 6**
5. What is a behavioral specialist? **Page # 11**
39. How do drills adhere to the treatment plan? **Page # 60**
40. How do drills relate to applied behavioral analysis? **Page # 62**
41. What is a discrete stimulus or SD? **Page # 64**
42. What is a target? **Page # 66**
68. After skills are mastered, how does a therapist generalize these to different settings? **Page # 107**

Training, and more training, and even more training

Issues regarding discrete trials and discrete stimulus and mastering targets can seem pretty daunting to students just beginning to consider a career working with special needs children. Even if you have already worked for years and are just now considering a change in careers, the specifics of implementing some programs may appear complicated and difficult. Don't worry!

Even with a four year degree, the additional training involved to take a position as a TSS or other role is substantial. The important thing is to get to know these terms and how they apply to the work as early as possible so that you can build a strong foundation.

What is a drill?

The therapist's main function is to help the client navigate through everyday activities without behavioral problems. Drills achieve this by helping to shape compliant behavior and motivate the client to process language. These skills, the ability to exhibit appropriate behavior in social situations and the ability to communicate functionally, set the foundation for the primary goal of delivering treatment to autistic children.

Each drill has a section in a child's treatment plan with a target list. A target is the focus of the drill. As targets are mastered, the focus changes. For example, if we want a child to follow the command, "touch square," we use, "square," as the target. After the client manages to touch a square upon command, the therapist may place this target with a number of false targets, such as circles, triangles, etc. Once the client shows the ability to pick the square out from numerous targets, the therapist continues with another change.

The treatment plan outlines what criteria need to be met for mastery, while also providing the series of targets to be mastered and in what way. Each drill is in its own section in the treatment plan and consists of:

1. A description of the drill - The drill is briefly described and the phases of the drill are listed.

2. A question or direction - The question or direction does not change. If the direction in the drill is listed as, "touch," then it is always, "touch." Consistency is extremely important to getting positive results, especially when more than one therapist works on the case.

3. A target list - The target list is the first page in the drill's section. The list includes the date that the target was introduced and when it was mastered. This page helps the team to quickly reference how long the child has been working on a target and how long it took him to master a target.

4. A percentage chart or graph - The therapist averages the number of correct responses and records the percent correct on a chart or graph. This helps the team to quickly assess the child's progress in the drill.

5. Data collection sheets or bubble sheets - The therapist records each of the child's responses to directions and questions. Bubble sheets are pages in the program book that help the therapist quickly record responses while continuing the drill at a steady pace.

A bubble sheet contains letters that correspond to possible responses from the child:

Correct = C; Incorrect = I; No Response = NR; Prompt = P

The letters are arranged in blocks of ten corresponding to the number of trials usually attempted in each drill. The TSS can quickly circle the appropriate letter according to the child's response. The TSS also writes the SD and the target on the bubble sheet as well as the percent correct. This information helps the next shift run smoother because the TSS knows what was done during the last shift.

Summary: The therapy provided for a special needs child is very structured. There are forms of treatment other than Wraparound (such as RDI and the Son-Rise program), but the dominant system offered through social services is Wraparound. Through this system, the behaviorist and case manager develop a treatment plan following ABA's use of Discrete Trial Drills. A therapist's job is to take this plan and put it into action. Much of their time is spent administering, evaluating and recording the results from drills.

It is very important to understand how these drills help the special needs child. Autisic and PDD children have difficulty learning socially. The condition also makes it difficult for the child to focus, to react to stimuli and engage in activities with others. As the therapist works through the drills developed in the treatment plan, they shape the child's behavior in such a way that makes it possible for them to successfully take part in a social environment.

Now, you might be wondering ....

1. What is a therapist (TSS)? **Page # 6**
9. What treatment program is used most frequently? **Page # 16**
28. What is applied behavioral analysis? **Page # 42**
29. What is behavior? **Page # 44**
37. What are the phases of discrete trial drills? **Page # 56**
39. How do drills adhere to the treatment plan? **Page # 60**
40. How do drills relate to applied behavioral analysis? **Page # 62**
41. What is a discrete stimulus or SD? **Page # 64**
42. What is a target? **Page # 66**
51. How do bubble sheets fit into the therapist's work? **Page # 80**
63. How does a therapist, 'shape,' behavior? **Page # 100**

QUESTION 39

How do drills adhere to the treatment plan?

When a treatment team meets to develop a plan for the child's therapy, they begin by determining exactly what they want therapy to achieve for the child. Starting with these goals, the behaviorist, case manager and therapist create, 'drills,' that will help work the child towards meeting the treatment plan's goals. Drills can be very simple or complex, ranging from having the child touch a piece of paper, to having them choose one specific toy out of a group of toys (these would be called targets).

Within the Wraparound program, drills serve a number of purposes. When developing drills, team members make certain that the actions work the child towards goals related to compliance, attention, communication and social skills. What follows are explanations for how these treatment goals relate to drills:

1. **Compliance** - Every drill addresses compliance goals by giving the child a direction to follow. The therapist uses rewards after each correct response to reinforce compliant behavior. Many new cases require a, "come sit," drill that focuses on the child following through with the command. Once the child sits, he is rewarded. Gradually, the rewards are faded out and the child simply sits when given the direction. All drills follow the same general format. The child complies. He is rewarded. The rewards are gradually faded out. The child has acquired a new skill.

2. **Attention** - Drills require the child to focus on the task at hand. When a therapist engages the child in a drill, she creates an environment that has little or no distractions. For example, if a therapist is engaging the child in a matching drill, she clears the work area of all other objects and focuses the child's attention on the materials used in the matching drill. She uses only enough words to convey what is expected. The child is rewarded for correct responses. Correct responses demonstrate that she is paying attention. The rewards are gradually faded. The child has attended long enough to demonstrate mastery.

3. **Communication** - In order to follow the therapist's instructions, the child has to be able to receive and process the information, and then demonstrate understanding through actions or words. If the child demonstrates understanding when the target is used in the stimulus, the child is using receptive processing skills. If the child demonstrates understanding when the target is not used in the stimulus, he is using expressive processing skills. For example, the therapist gives the command, "show me book," in a sign language drill and the child signs, "book." He receptively processed the word *book* and demonstrated understanding through action. If the therapist holds a book saying, "what is this?" and the child signs, "book," the child is using expressive processing skills.

4. **Social skills** - Drills also address social goals. The child will look to the therapist for consequences for his responses. A common early drill is eye contact in which the child is directed to look at the therapist. Gradually the therapist prompts the child to sustain eye contact for longer increments of time. Drills help the child develop an understanding of reciprocal interaction and cause-and-effect relationships.

Even though each child is unique and therapy differs from case to case, drills usually follow the same format. Sometimes a drill needs to be varied according to the child's progress.

Summary - Drills are the foundation of Applied Behavioral Analysis. Much of a therapist's time during a session is spent initiating and recording the results of drills. The main two components of a drill are the stimulus (Discrete Stimulus or SD) and the target. The stimulus describes an action. The target describes the object that the client must act upon.

When a therapist runs drills, the goal is not to teach the child how to touch a square or circle. The therapist is teaching the client to interact with and respond to another individual. Throughout this process, the therapist records data pertaining to the engagement and this information is used by the behavioral specialist to follow the progress of therapy and make necessary changes.

Now, you might be wondering ....

36. What are discrete trials? **Page # 54**
37. What are the phases of discrete trial drills? **Page # 56**
38. What is a drill? **Page # 58**
40. How do drills relate to applied behavioral analysis? **Page # 62**
41. What is a discrete stimulus or SD? **Page # 64**
42. What is a target? **Page # 66**
43. How is a target introduced? **Page # 67**
44. What if a child can not master a target? **Page # 68**
45. What is random rotation? **Page # 69**
46. What are receptive & expressive processing drills? **Page # 71**
47. What is the difference between sign language and receptive processing drills? **Page # 72**
48. How does a therapist use sign language in drills? **Page # 73**
49. What is the treatment plan? **Page # 76**
51. How do bubble sheets fit into the therapist's work? **Page # 80**
52. What does a target list look like? **Page # 82**
63. How does a therapist, 'shape,' behavior? **Page # 100**
93. What are some important moments in applied behavioral analysis? **Page # 148**
94. What are some methods for autism treatment aside from ABA? **Page # 150**

QUESTION 40: How do discrete trial drills relate to ABA?

ABA (Applied Behavioral Analysis) has roots in the behaviorist splinter of Psychology. The approach focuses on rewarding positive behavior and discounting negative behavior. ABA breaks a task down into small steps. As the child masters each step another one is introduced. This approach is effective for individuals who have difficulty staying focused. Applied Behavioral Analysis also uses positive and negative reinforcement to motivate the client. Different agencies will use different materials, but the underlying concepts of Applied Behavior Analysis are prevalent in the drills.

1. **The drill is applied.** The skill acquired through performing the drill should have social significance. The skills addressed in the drill will depend on the child's treatment plan. For example, one treatment plan may expect the client to follow directions, make eye contact and remain focused to a specific task for increasing periods of time. These skills relate to compliance (following directions), social skills (making eye contact) and attention goals (focusing on a task).

2. **The drill is behavioral.** The therapist records objective data. For example, throughout a course of drills, the therapist may count the number of times the child requires a prompt and how much time elapsed between being presented with a stimulus and getting a reaction.

3. **The drill is analytic.** The data collected should reflect that the interventions used in the drill result in a change in the child's behavior. For example, if you were working with a child who was non-compliant, the collected data would show that after a course of drills they follow directions. The data may also show the average number of prompts needed to get the correct behavior and how long therapy took to reach this milestone.

4. **The drill is methodical.** The techniques that one uses should be described in enough detail that another therapist can duplicate the drill without direct supervision. Any therapist should be able to open a program book and pick up right where the last one finished. This is done through the target list, data sheets and bubble sheets.

5. **The drill is conceptually systematic**. The drills follow established behavioral approaches. For example, a drill uses principals of operant conditioning in order to reinforce appropriate behavior. The child is rewarded for positive behavior. This system of positive and negative rewards follow specific steps that the therapist controls and the child comes to understand through therapy.

6. **The drill is effective.** The data collected should reflect that there is a significant change in the child's behavior.

7. **The drill can be generalized.** The child's change in behavior should be evident in general settings. For example, if the therapist was working with the child to respond to the word, "wait," after a certain period of time, the client should wait when told at home, in school and on a playground.

Now, you might be wondering ....

28. What is applied behavioral analysis? **Page # 42**
29. What is behavior? **Page # 44**
37. What are the phases of discrete trial drills? **Page # 56**
63. How does a therapist, 'shape,' behavior? **Page # 100**
98. Where can I go to learn more about educational programs related to working with special needs children? **Page # 156**
100. I think I want to work with special needs children, where should I start? **Page # 159**

A little on the empirical sciences

There are a number of ways to describe Applied Behavioral Analysis, how it relates to programs such as Wraparound and also how it relates to the science of Behaviorism.

All of these things are the result of empirical science. Empiricism is the philosophy that supports the scientific method. This school of thought is guided by the idea that an explanation (hypothesis) for a natural event must be able to be tested, the event must be observable and test results must be able to be reproduced by others in order for the event to be able to be properly studied.

One way to look at Applied Behavioral Analysis is as the group of methods developed from years of scientific testing, with the methods for this testing guided by empiricism.

QUESTION 41

What is a discrete stimulus or SD?

SD stands for discriminative stimulus. Like the term, *discrete trial*, the term's roots are in Behaviorism. A drill is comprised of the discriminative stimulus and the target.

When a therapist works with a child, they use the discriminative stimulus as the initial direction or question that requires a response from the child. When the child gives the correct response they receive a reward. Hopefully, the child makes a pleasurable connection between the SD, the desired response and the reward.

To keep drills simple, the discriminative stimulus usually consists of only one or two words. When introducing a new discriminative stimulus, the therapist may use visual or physical prompts to help the child process what is expected. The initial prompt may be followed by a reward to encourage the child to repeat the desired response.

Therapists find the SD on the target list in the drill section of the child's program book. This helps the therapist to consistently use the same one or two word SD connected with the drill. If the SD is, "touch," the therapist simply uses the word, "touch," followed by the target. If the target is a square, the SD, "touch," would precede square. The therapist would repeat ten trials of, "touch square," and record the child's response to each trial.

Common discriminative stimuli include:

1. **Match** - Targets are usually introduced through matching. Matching is visual and it is a relatively easy skill for the child to master.

2. **Touch** - *Touch* is another fundamental direction. It is an action that is in most cases easily acquired because it is visual and requires only one step.

3. **Give** - *Give* is a little more complex because it involves steps. The child must first process the direction (stimulus), then pick up the appropriate item and hand it to the therapist. *Give* is a valuable skill for the child to learn because it can be generalized into a number of different settings.

4. **Point to** - Pointing is a little more complex because it requires the child to process the stimulus, form his hand into a pointing pose and point to the appropriate item. Pointing requires some fine motor skill.

5. **Do this** - A therapist uses this SD in nonverbal imitation drills. This SD is found in many new cases and lower-functioning cases.

6. **Say** - This SD is used in verbal imitation drills. Verbal imitation drills begin with sounds and eventually lead to words.

Now, you might be wondering ....

28. What is applied behavioral analysis? **Page # 42**
29. What is behavior? **Page # 44**
37. What are the phases of discrete trial drills? **Page # 56**
98. Where can I go to learn more about educational programs related to working with special needs children? **Page # 156**
100. I think I want to work with special needs children, where should I start? **Page # 159**

How long do treatment programs last?

The Wraparound program is short term. Generally, any program that involves taking treatment to the client is going to be temporary. The clients that are served through these services usually have less severe behavioral issues and are not overly aggressive.

In contrast, on-going programs take place in residential facilities or hospitals. Professionals that work in these areas may work with one child throughout the entire course of their education. In many residential programs a child's aggression, or severe symptoms, make it impossible for them to remain with the family. Therapists in these situations can spend years working with the same patients, addressing the same problems for months and even years to progress slowly forward.

As you make career decisions related to working with special needs children, it is important that you take differences such as these into consideration. Doing so will help you to find the type of work environment best suited to you.

QUESTION 42

What is a target? What significance do they have in therapy?

When a therapist works with an autistic child, they go through drills. A drill involves giving the child a disciminative stimulus. This would be a command or request, such as the word, "touch." The therapist also gives a target, which is the focus of the SD (SD is the abbreviation used for discriminative stimulus). An example of a target would be a square piece of paper or a specific toy.

A target is not the *goal* of the drill. Drills are designed to shape behavior. They are not designed to be academic. A target has significance in the drill because the child is required to demonstrate that he is following directions and that he is attending to the task. Mastering letters, shapes and numbers is actually incidental to the drill. The primary goals always relate to the child's treatment plan and commonly involve improving attention, compliance, communication and/or social skills.

At the start of therapy, a target is introduced in isolation. For example, if the SD is, "touch," and the target is a square, the therapist places a square in front of the child and says, "touch square." The child responds, while the worker gives the child immediate feedback. There is nothing to distract the child when the target is presented in isolation. Once the child masters the target in isolation, this is recorded in the child's program book in the target list.

After a target is mastered in isolation, the therapist moves to the next step. This varies according to the child's program. A *distractor* may be introduced, or the target may be put into *random rotation*. Most programs use the latter, but in some cases using a distracter first is very helpful in getting better results.

A distracter is anything that is used to distract the child from the target. The distracter forces the child to discriminate between the two items in the drill. The distracter initially has very different characteristics from the target. For example, I would use a picture of an animal as a distracter for a color. When I give the direction, "touch blue," the child must discriminate between the animal and the color. Once the child masters the target when a distracter is used, the target is put into random rotation.

The target is considered mastered when the child is able to give the appropriate response to the direction in random rotation a certain percent of the trials. The percent correct necessary to achieve mastery depends on the case, but it usually is 80% or higher.

Now, you might be wondering ....

43. How is a target introduced? **Page # 67**

What are some methods that a therapist uses to acquaint the child to targets?

QUESTION 43

The process normally starts with performing drills to help children match targets. A target can be anything from a picture of a blue circle to one of the child's toys. Matching helps the child become familiar with the targets because of the visual component. An autistic child tends to think in pictures making this an ideal discriminative stimulus that works with the child's early strengths.

After the child becomes familiar with matching, the skill will be used as a starting point for introducing unfamiliar targets. At first, the child matches identical pictures, letters, numbers, shapes or objects. The new target is repeated over and over throughout the drill and the child gradually becomes familiar with the word that relates to the target. The sound of someone saying, "blue," will eventually be linked to the color blue.

More complex matching drills may be introduced into the child's program. Eventually, the behavior specialist may design a drill that requires the child to match a three-dimensional object to a picture.

Categorizing is one example of a more complex matching drill. The child matches according to category. In a categorizing drill, the SD is usually, "put with." This SD helps the child transition from matching identical items to putting similar items into categories.

One of my favorite complex matching drills requires the child to match an item with an object or activity. For example, the child is directed to match a tire to a car or crayons to a picture of someone coloring. I like to link the drill with a play activity. These more complex matching activities are usually introduced after or along with receptive processing drills.

The drill is elevated to receptive processing after the child masters matching a series of targets. The child learns to receptively process the discriminative stimulus and target in order to provide a response. Receptive processing does not require the child to give a verbal response.

Now, you might be wondering ....

42. What is a target? **Page # 66**
44. What if a child can not master a target? **Page # 68**
45. What is random rotation? **Page # 69**
46. What are receptive & expressive processing drills? **Page # 71**

QUESTION 44

What if a client can not master a target?

Some targets are quickly mastered and others are stumbling blocks for the client. If a target is not mastered in a reasonable number of trials, it is put on hold and another target is introduced. Sometimes an entire drill may be put on hold if the child does not seem to be grasping it. The therapist may periodically test the target to see if the child is ready to work with it again.

I've found that taking a break from difficult parts of therapy is often all that is needed. I worked with a girl who simply could not comprehend colors. She would just randomly touch the colors during the drill. Many times, she wouldn't even look at the colors as she made her choice. After months of performing this drill, we finally put the entire color drill on hold. A few months later, I put the red and black cards in front of her, gave the command and she immediately gave the correct response. She had all of the colors listed as targets in her treatment plan mastered within weeks.

I've also seen targets that are quickly mastered in isolation, but are not mastered in random rotation. Many times the child has difficulty discriminating. The child is able to follow the stimulus, but can't discriminate between targets. This is a big obstacle in any drill but there are ways to work through it.

I may have the client practice the targets in isolation a little longer. Some targets require more repetition than others. The child may not find the target particularly interesting or motivating and she may lose focus. I may make a target a little more interesting by using motivating rewards. M&Ms are good. They may be the motivation the child needs to master the normally uninteresting target.

When I face problems, I always try to get creative. Sometimes I use the target throughout the shift. If the child is not mastering a letter, I use an alphabet puzzle to reinforce the letter. The child may love to color. Draw the letter and instruct the child to color it while repeating the letter and praising her work. If the child likes songs, sing the alphabet song. Emphasize the targeted letter and show the letter to the child as you sing. There are countless ways of reinforcing a target throughout the shift and many therapists find that this is an area where some creativity is very helpful.

Now, you might be wondering ....

36. What are discrete trials? **Page # 54**
38. What is a drill? **Page # 58**
42. What is a target? **Page # 66**

What is random rotation?

QUESTION 45

Random rotation is when the therapist places two targets that were each previously mastered on the table or work station and directs the child to discriminate between the two. The therapist then randomly changes the position of the targets and repeats the discriminative stimulus. The target used in the direction is also changed. Random rotation takes practice, but it eventually runs very smoothly.

Targets that are acquired in isolation or with a distracter are not considered completely mastered until they are achieved in random rotation. A drill must have at least two targets mastered in isolation or with a distracter before it can be put into random rotation.

When using random rotation, a therapist will:

1. **Consistently use the same SD** - The discriminative stimulus is not randomly rotated. The child may become very confused if the SD and the targets are both rotated. Usually, this would be too much for the child to process.

2. **Change the position of the target** - The child may memorize the position of the targets. If the targets do not change positions during the drill, they are not really in random rotation.

3. **Change the target used with the SD** - The targets need to be changed in order to assure that the child is really discriminating.

4. **Try not to accidentally prompt the child** - A therapist can easily give away the right target when exercising a drill in random rotation. Therapists tend to unintentionally do this by always putting the correct target on the right. It is also not uncommon for a therapist to glance at the correct target while giving the direction

The key to random rotation is changing position and targets. Let's say a client has mastered the color blue and the color orange in isolation. The next step according to the child's treatment plan and program book is to put the colors into random rotation. The drill would follow a format like this:

1. The therapist places the two colors side-by-side in front of the client
2. The therapist says, "Touch blue."
3. The child responds by touching the appropriate color
4. The response is rewarded
5. The therapist picks up the colors and changes their position
6. The child responds correctly and is rewarded
7. The therapist says, "Touch yellow."

8. The child responds incorrectly
9. The therapist does not change the position of the target
10. The therapist says, "Touch yellow."

Random rotation is a fairly thorough means of determining whether or not a target is mastered. Once the list of targets is mastered, the drill moves on to the next phase.

Now, you might be wondering ....

36. What are discrete trials? **Page # 54**
37. What are the phases of discrete trial drills? **Page # 56**
38. What is a drill? **Page # 58**
39. How do drills adhere to the treatment plan? **Page # 60**
40. How do drills relate to applied behavioral analysis? **Page # 62**
41. What is a discrete stimulus or SD? **Page # 64**
42. What is a target? **Page # 66**

Understanding the treatment plan

The treatment plan that a team develops for a client in the Wraparound program is of central importance to reaching therapeutic goals. Not only does the initial plan provide the team with the direction needed to create individual sessions that address very specific goals. As the sessions progress, data is collected and reviewed, changes to the plan are made and the client continues to receive ever more focused attention.

As you can see, the idea of *treatment as a process* is closely connected to the way that a team is constantly gathering data and making changes to the client's plan for treatment.

What are receptive & expressive processing drills?

QUESTION 46

Receptive processing drills are used to teach the child to follow spoken directions. These drills usually require the child to identify an object, letter, shape or color. The SD, "touch," is commonly used in receptive processing drills. Other SD's include, "give," and "point to." The child has to be able to follow the commands in order to engage in the drill. For example, a prerequisite for the SD, "give me square," would be for the child to give an item to another person. The same goes for pointing. If the child has not learned how to give or point, the therapist uses, "touch," because it is the most visual and easiest to acquire.

Receptive Processing - Receptive processing requires the child to interpret the SD and identify the target. After clients have mastered matching skills, they are taught to receptively identify the target. If the targets have been randomly rotated, they should be familiar to the child. This helps the child transition into a receptive processing drill.

Receptive processing is analogous to multiple choice questions on an exam. The child demonstrates that he recognizes the correct response but does not have to explain it in words.

Expressive Processing - Expressive processing is analogous to an essay question. The child is required to interpret the stimulus, identify the target and produce the word that corresponds to the target. Not all clients are able to engage in expressive processing drills because they all have not acquired language.

A common discriminative stimulus in an expressive drill is, "what ____?" The target is not included in the direction because the child uses the word associated with the target in his response. For example, if the target is, 'cow,' the SD would be, "what animal?" and the child's targeted response would be, "cow." Seem simple? It can take months of work to get a client to this point.

Children who are nonverbal can engage in expressive drills. The child may learn signs that represent objects, colors, shapes or nearly any target. If the child has the ability to sign accurately, he can move on to the expressive phase of the drill. A typical sign language drill is not expressive, though.

Now, you might be wondering ....

38. What is a drill? **Page # 58**
41. What is a discrete stimulus or SD? **Page # 64**

QUESTION 47

What is the difference between sign language and receptive processing drills?

Before answering this question, I want to touch on why it is important to ask it. Regardless of the type of program a professional works with, from the popular Wraparound programs, to something administered through a residential facility, a large part of your job is going to be documenting behavior as data. The therapist on a treatment team would be the one spending the most time making the actual documentation, but the behaviorist and case manager also spend time reading that data, analyzing and working with it. It is very important, early on, regardless of your position, to begin thinking of drills and their corresponding parts, along with the child's behaviors, in terms that can be recorded. In this profession, the *meaning* of a behavior is secondary to the *objective* ways in which you can describe it. This question is one of those areas where many people just getting started get a little confused.

A good way to demonstrate the difference is through example. A common receptive processing drill is *Receptive Commands*. During a receptive command drill, a therapist uses the *skill* as the stimulus (SD). For example, if the target is *clap*, the therapist says, "clap," in the drill. The child receptively processes the word and demonstrates understanding through action. The child has to summon the action from memory.

During a sign language drill, the therapist uses the specific sign in the SD. For example, if the target sign is *book*, the therapist uses the SD, "show me book." The child receptively processes the word, "book," and demonstrates understanding through using the sign that correlates with a book.

The difference, then, is that a receptive processing drill focuses on skills and expects an action to demonstate the skill. Sign language drills focus on communication and understanding.

Summary - Does this seem like a pretty small point? I've found this to be a rewarding, and very often enjoyable, career, but these points are the work of it. There are many subtleties to the job. In order for the team to communicate efficiently everyone needs to have the same understanding of behavior, drills and a thorough understanding of the terms used in therapy.

Now, you might be wondering ....

36. What are discrete trials? **Page # 54**
38. What is a drill? **Page # 58**
41. What is a discrete stimulus or SD? **Page # 64**
42. What is a target? **Page # 66**

How does a therapist use sign language?

QUESTION 48

Sign language is a very useful tool for communication. It is visual and many autistic children learn visual skills quickly. Nonverbal autistic children tend to get frusterated easily. Learning a method of communication not only helps facilitate therapy, but helps the child lessen frusteration by giving them an outlet for expression. In all, this can be a very important skill for a special needs child to learn.

Therapists do not need to be fluent in sign language. When I started working as a therapist, I knew the signs for the letters in the alphabet and the sign for, "I don't know."

Signs commonly used in therapy are:

1. **More** - More is one of the most important signs for a child to learn because it makes the abstract concrete. For example, I can't really use a picture that clearly represents, "more," but I can engage a child in a very rewarding activity, like swinging, and prompt the child to sign *more* to continue swinging. They pick that one up pretty quickly.

2. **Help** - Help is a great sign to use because it helps the child communicate that a task is too difficult before he becomes frustrated. I like to use puzzles to reinforce the sign for help. If the child is struggling with the puzzle, I use a prompt to help the child sign and I say, "help," as we make the motions together. I immediately help the child put the piece into the puzzle.

3. **All done** - This is a very motivational sign but it needs to be used with caution. Often, the child will quickly associate, "all done," with finishing therapy for the day. It is best to save this sign for the end of the shift until the child is able to generalize it. I once prompted a child to sign, "all done," when we were only a few minutes into the session and the child ran out of the therapy room with joy. It was pretty hard to get him back in the room.

The team may also choose signs that represent motivational objects or activities. If the child loves to look at books, the team would include the sign, "book," in the child's program. Therapists also use sign language when giving directions or praise.

Now, you might be wondering ....

36. What are discrete trials? **Page # 54**
38. What is a drill? **Page # 58**
41. What is a discrete stimulus or SD? **Page # 64**

Summary - Therapy

Treatment programs exist for the sole purpose of bringing therapy to a client. Whether it takes place in a residential facility where special needs children live full time, in a special school, or in the child's home as is done in Wraparound, the various programs are all designed to facilitate treatment. Every role within a team is going to in some way support the sessions that take place between the special needs child and the therapist. For this reason, regardless of your role, understanding the specifics of therapy is crucial.

Therapy normally involves communication between the therapist and client, where discrete stimuli are offered (questions or commands). These are normally connected to a target - the object and desired response that are the focus of the drill. As the client progresses, becoming more capable of satisfying the goals of the drills, therapy is altered, usually becoming more difficult, to teach more complicated skills or combine already mastered skills. All of these drills are guided by the treatment plan developed by the team. This is, in turn, guided by data collected by the therapist during sessions.

Your Questions Answered on... TOOLS FOR THERAPY

49. What is the treatment plan? **Page # 76**

50. What is the crisis plan? **Page # 78**

51. How do bubble sheets fit into the therapist's work? **Page # 80**

52. What does a target list look like? **Page # 82**

53. What is a visual treatment schedule? **Page # 84**

54. What is an ABC chart? **Page # 86**

55. What is a token economy system? **Page # 88**

56. What is an incident report? **Page # 90**

57. What is a maintenance program? **Page # 92**

58. What is a Picture Exchange Communication System and how is it used? **Page # 93**

59. What is the program book? **Page # 94**

QUESTION 49: What is a treatment plan?

Before ever receiving treatment, a client is seen by a psychiatrist. If the psychiatrist deems it necessary, she will prescribe a specific number of treatment hours to the child or adolescent. The parents choose an agency to handle their child's case and the agency organizes a team to work on the case.

The team consists of a case manager, behavior therapist and a group of therapists (sometimes called therapeutic support staff workers). The behavior specialist develops the client's treatment plan in collaboration with the family, using the child's diagnosis, strengths and needs as a starting point. The family identifies specific areas of concern with the child's behavior, communication and social skills. The treatment plan addresses these problems by stating the child's needs, what goals are to be reached, what interventions are going to be used and what outcomes are expected.

Strengths Section - The strengths section of the treatment plan includes the child's attributes and likes. It describes the child and gives a general idea of the child's nature. This information helps the team choose motivators to use during therapy. The strengths section also includes other important information about the child's background including where he lives and who lives with him. It may also hint at the family's involvement in the child's therapy.

The child's abilities may also be included in the strengths section. If the treatment plan states that the child is compliant and sustains eye contact, the therapist would recognize that the child is ready to follow directions at a work station and that the child has some social skills.

Needs Section - The needs section of the treatment plan briefly lists the areas in which the child needs to improve. These needs are then translated into goals. Common needs found in a treatment plan are ***attention, communication, compliance, play skills*** and ***social skills.*** Many of the needs overlap. For example, the need to improve play skills may involve attention, communication and compliance. Each need is described in one or two sentences.

Progress Section - The overall progress/change the child makes through therapy is addressed in its own section. This section briefly covers the child's progress over the previous four months of treatment. The team will set aside time to review this every four months and the treatment plan and programs are adjusted according to the child's success or lack of success with the interventions. The progress section uses the data collected by the therapist to measure the client's advancement in the program. This section includes information about the client's attainment of goals, skills and anything relevant to the child's progress.

As the child reaches his goals in the treatment plan, Wraparound services are gradually faded out. Each treatment plan includes a fade plan. The fade plan is very specific and it spells out what the child will be able to do by the time the fade plan goes into effect. The services are gradually reduced according to the fade plan's specifications.

Crisis Plan - The final section of the treatment plan is the crisis plan. The crisis plan lists actions to be taken when the client's behavior is out of control. The crisis plan is used only when the client is at risk of harming himself, harming others or if he may damage property.

Now, you might be wondering ....

9. What treatment program is used most frequently? **Page # 16**
36. What are discrete trials? **Page # 54**
37. What are the phases of discrete trial drills? **Page # 56**
38. What is a drill? **Page # 58**
40. How do drills relate to applied behavioral analysis? **Page # 62**
50. What is the crisis plan? **Page # 78**
51. How do bubble sheets fit into the therapist's work? **Page # 80**
56. What is an incident report? **Page # 90**
57. What is a maintenance program? **Page # 92**

Do all programs use the same kind of treatment plan?

Most treatment programs establish goals early on and use the same kind of review system that you find in a Wraparound program. However, not all programs are based on sessions that involve the use of drills, which greatly impacts the role of the therapist. For example, DIR Floortime runs in a completely different direction from Wraparound, with daily sessions managed by the child's natural motivations. The therapist works according to goals and follows a program, but it is a much different experience working in this atmosphere.

You can learn more about different programs on **Page # 150**.

What is the crisis plan?

QUESTION 50

When it comes to working on-site as a therapist, one of the first things you must master is how to create an environment conducive to learning. Whether you are working with an autistic child or troubled adolescent, you must be skilled in managing the behavior of the client to create and maintain that desired environment. Techniques for this are covered in the overall treatment plan, developed by the behaviorist.

The crisis plan, as a part of the treatment plan, outlines specific actions the therapist, family and school should take if the child's behavior gets out of control and disturbs treatment. Many of the strategies found in a typical treatment plan are included in the *Safe Crisis Management Technique* training.

Each Crisis plan is tailored to the individual client, but many draw on the following strategies:

1. Redirection - One effective strategy for handling disruptive behavior is redirection. Redirection is simply getting the child to focus on another activity. If the child is poking at a therapist, the therapist would immediately redirect the child's attention. This can be done by using words or visual distractions. This strategy is effective for nearly all levels of functioning. If a high functioning child is making nasty remarks, the therapist would simply draw the child's attention to another topic without satisfying the remark with a response.

2. Ignoring - Ignoring is another effective strategy similar to redirection. Behavior is essentially communication, and each behavior has a specific purpose. Sometimes a child will exhibit a negative behavior simply for a response. If no response is given, the behavior often ceases. I worked with a child who purposely gave incorrect responses because she liked to hear me say, "nope." She would smile each time that I used the word. I found that, "try again," worked better because the phrase was not reinforcing.

3. Environmental Controls - Some behavior can not be ignored or redirected. These behaviors are ***non-negotiable*** and include any behavior that endangers the therapist or the client. Environmental controls are often used when dealing with non-negotiable behaviors. When using environmental controls, a therapist may move the client to another area of the room, or the therapist may remove himself from the area. In either case, the change should not be desirable. Once the negative behavior ceases, the environment is returned to normal. This may not seem like a very strict strategy, but it can be very effective for autistic children that are sensitive to their environment or crave order.

The crisis plan section of the treatment plan is not an actual goal for the child to reach. It is a standard section that provides practical strategies for dealing with extreme behavior. The therapy is, for the most part, based entirely on specific goals, but the Crisis plan and the strategies that a therapist uses through *Safe Crisis Management Technique*, are important for creating an environment that allows therapeutic goals to be achieved

Now, you might be wondering ....

36. What are discrete trials? **Page # 54**
37. What are the phases of discrete trial drills? **Page # 56**
38. What is a drill? **Page # 58**
40. How do drills relate to applied behavioral analysis? **Page # 62**
50. What is the crisis plan? **Page # 78**
51. How do bubble sheets fit into the therapist's work? **Page # 80**
56. What is an incident report? **Page # 90**
57. What is a maintenance program? **Page # 92**
58. What is a Picture Exchange Communication System and how is it used? **Page # 93**

Maintaining the therapeutic environment

The crisis plan is a crucial part of therapy that relates to a much larger issue. The therapist and family in any treatment program must create an environment where the client can effectively work through sessions. Even in a program such as Relationship Development Intervention, which uses a much more relaxed environment than Wraparound, creating the right environment and then maintaining it, is of the highest importance.

As you can see from the types of categories covered in the Crisis plan, this instrument of treatment is geared towards putting controls in place that let the therapist know how to react when they encounter disruptive behavior. Mastering effective strategies for keeping the treatment environment under control is a major part of the therapist's work and one of those skills that sets them apart.

QUESTION 51
How do bubble sheets fit into a therapist's work?

Bubble sheets are convenient pages in a program book that help the therapist quickly record the child's responses and actions as objective data that is later reviewed by a behaviorist. The way that bubble sheets are designed allows for the therapist to continue activities at a steady and continuous pace.

Bubble sheets are a very important part of therapy because the data recorded on these is taken back to the treatment team and used to make changes to the treatment plan to help that specific child in areas where he or she is having problems.

A bubble sheet contains letters that correspond to possible responses from the child:

Correct = C; Incorrect = I; No Response = NR; Prompt = P

The letters are arranged in blocks of ten corresponding to the number of trials (usually) attempted in each drill. The therapist can quickly circle the appropriate letter according to the child's response. The therapist also writes the stimulus (SD) and the target on the bubble sheet as well as the percent correct. This information helps the next shift run smoother because the therapist knows what was done during the last shift.

Bubble sheets look something like this:

SD: Touch
Target: Square Introduced in isolation
Date: 1\06\05
Initials: TR

C	I	NR	P
C	I	NR	P
C	I	NR	P

How bubble sheets relate to Applied Behavioral Analysis and Wraparound:

The Wraparound program is currently the most popular, standardized, treatment program for autistic and PDD children in the United States. The Wraparound program is based on Applied Behavioral Analysis (ABA), a set a methodologies based on the Behaviorist school of thought. ABA uses strict empirical methods to reach specific goals. Actions and consequences must be recorded using objective means.

Considering that a therapist goes through dozens of drills in the course of a session (meaning hundreds of individual trials), well designed tools are a necessary part of providing therapy. Bubble sheets are simple, but incredibly effective, data collection tools that a therapist quickly learns to use in order to record information that other team members use to review and change the plan for treatment.

Now, you might be wondering ....

9. What treatment program is used most frequently? **Page # 16**
36. What are discrete trials? **Page # 54**
37. What are the phases of discrete trial drills? **Page # 56**
38. What is a drill? **Page # 58**
40. How do drills relate to applied behavioral analysis? **Page # 62**
41. What is a discrete stimulus or SD? **Page # 64**
42. What is a target? **Page # 66**
50. What is the crisis plan? **Page # 78**
56. What is an incident report? **Page # 90**
57. What is a maintenance program? **Page # 92**
58. What is a Picture Exchange Communication System and how is it used? **Page # 93**
59. What is the program book? **Page # 94**

Okay, so...

You may be wondering how important it is to know this. If you are just starting to consider this field, you don't have to worry too much about how these sheets work. However, you should be concerned with understanding the ideology behind them. Bubble sheets are nothing more than data collection sheets (it's just that we call them bubble sheets). If you are thinking of this type of field as a career, you'll want to get some exposure to the sciences so that you understand how and why objective data is gathered.

QUESTION 52

What does a target list look like?

As a therapist, you become very familiar with target lists. Once you learn the steps to discrete trial, you will be able to navigate through the forms with no trouble. A target list helps the treatment team keep track of the child's progress in a drill. In a quick glance, the treatment team can see what targets the child has mastered and how long it took for him to master the targets.

A target list usually looks something like this:

Drill: Receptive Shapes
SD: "Touch _____"
Response: Child touches appropriate shape
Mastery = 80% - 100% correct

Target RR	Introduced	Mastered Isolation	Mastered
Square	1/06/05	1/10/05	1/18/05
Circle	1/11/05	1/13/05	1/18/05
Triangle	1/19/05		

The treatment team gets important information from the target list about the child's progress. This child has mastered two shapes. He mastered the two shapes over a course of twelve days. Note that the date the first target was mastered matches the date that the second target was mastered. This is because the square and the circle were randomly rotated. The square was mastered in isolation, but could not be rotated with anything until a second shape was mastered. There would be nothing to rotate with square. Some target lists leave the date of the first target's random rotation column blank.

The treatment team can also determine what target is on acquisition by referring to the target list. In the example above, the target the child is acquiring is a triangle. All we know from the target list is the date that the shape was introduced. Since there is no date under *Mastered in Isolation*, the treatment team can assume that the child is still working on the triangle shape in isolation. Once the triangle is mastered in isolation, the treatment team moves the triangle into random rotation.

The shape will be rotated with circle and square. However, there will only be two shapes in front of the child at a time. The child will not have to discriminate between all of the shapes at once. There are some instances in which a child will discriminate between more than two items. These instances are case-specific according to the child's abilities and needs. For example, if the treatment team wants to develop the child's scanning abilities; they could have the child touch a familiar item that is among a number of distracting items. However, the structure of most drills follows the same format.

In order for the treatment team to see exactly what the child accomplished in the drill during his last few sessions, the team needs to refer to the data collection sheets or bubble sheets.

Now, you might be wondering ....

9. What treatment program is used most frequently? **Page #16**
28. What is applied behavioral analysis? **Page #42**
29. What is behavior? **Page #44**
36. What are discrete trials? **Page #54**
37. What are the phases of discrete trial drills? **Page #56**
38. What is a drill? **Page #58**
40. How do drills relate to applied behavioral analysis? **Page #62**
42. What is a target? **Page #66**
51. How do bubble sheets fit into the therapist's work? **Page #80**
58. What is a Picture Exchange Communication System and how is it used? **Page #93**
59. What is the program book? **Page #94**
63. How does a therapist, 'shape,' behavior? **Page #100**

Okay, so...

When it comes to therapy, actual targets are not the goals. It isn't really all that important that an autistic child can touch a rectangle or circle.

It's when the child shows understanding through an action that the treatment is proved successful. Also, engaging and following directions from another person is a sign of progression. The targets are just tools to facilitate these achievements.

QUESTION 53

What is a visual treatment schedule?

A visual treatment schedule is a collection of pictures representing activities that can be used to create a visual agenda for the session's activities that helps the therapist organize the shift. It also helps the child transition between activities by giving them a visual representation of their activities to reference.

The behavior specialist provides pictures that correspond with the drills in the child's treatment plan. With some practice, the child learns what each picture represents. The schedule is also a good tool for motivation. A child will often work diligently on a task if he understands that a preferred activity follows.

The visual schedule helps a child deal with unusual changes in a session as well. For example, I worked with a girl that ate dinner immediately following therapy. After dinner, she was finished for the day. She was very anxious to have free time and the regular schedule worked very well. On one occasion we had to change her schedule and she had to go back into the therapy room after eating. This kind of change in the schedule would normally cause negative behavior. I put a picture for, 'eat,' on the schedule followed by an image representing a computer activity. I chose a computer activity because it was the child's favorite. To my surprise, the child went straight into the therapy room after her meal with no prompting. She put away the meal icon and replaced it with the one for a computer. She then sat at her desk in front of the computer.

This example illustrates the importance of using visuals to facilitate communication as well as the power of motivation. The child had made a very strong connection to the picture of the computer and understood what it represented. Since it was her favorite activity, she eagerly re-entered the therapy room without incident. If I had chosen the picture for work, she probably would have tried to avoid entering the therapy room again. When it comes to working with special needs children, the therapist needs to develop a sense for these types of subtleties. Understanding what will motivate the child is absolutely necessary in order to deliver successful therapy.

The child's schedule can be organized on a visual treatment schedule either vertically or from left to right. Some argue that a vertical schedule is easier for a child to reference because it is organized like a list and people commonly scan from top to bottom. However, some argue that organizing the schedule from left to right helps the child with pre-reading skills. It is important to learn how to scan from left to right. I have found that each case is different and the best way to organize the schedule depends on the child. Some children can handle several tasks on a horizontal schedule while some function best on a vertical schedule with just two or three tasks.

A visual schedule commonly has three or four activities followed by a break, then three or four more tasks followed by, "All Done." I have found that most children learn **All Done** very quickly because it is very motivating. It is wise to sandwich a difficult task in between two preferred tasks. This often helps the child complete the difficult task without incident.

Visual schedules are a powerful tool, because they use pictures to help the child process language. With practice, the child begins to associate the spoken word with the picture and eventually the spoken word with the activity.

Now, you might be wondering ....

9. What treatment program is used most frequently? **Page # 16**
12. What are autism & PDD? **Page # 21**
28. What is applied behavioral analysis? **Page # 42**
29. What is behavior? **Page # 44**
36. What are discrete trials? **Page # 54**
37. What are the phases of discrete trial drills? **Page # 56**
38. What is a drill? **Page # 58**
40. How do drills relate to applied behavioral analysis? **Page # 62**
50. What is the crisis plan? **Page # 78**
51. How do bubble sheets fit into the therapist's work? **Page # 80**
58. What is a Picture Exchange Communication System and how is it used? **Page # 93**

Visual Systems

Visual stimuli for an autistic or PDD child can lead to some very interesting behaviors. An autistic child may become fascinated with moving objects, with lines in a drawing or the edge of a table. A child may also become overwhelmed by images, objects or colors. In some circumstances, the child's visual abilities will be extremely heightened, making them able to remember complex physical arrangements or solve intricate puzzles with ease.

QUESTION 54

What is an ABC chart?

An ABC chart is a form that a therapist uses to collect data on problem behaviors or any behavior that needs to be addressed through the treatment program. ABC stands for *antecedent, behavior* and *consequence.*

The ABC chart is normally broken into categories, specifying what information to include in each of these. For example, one data sheet may ask for the duration of the behavior. Another may include the time of day. The information required is determined by the behavior specialist and is usually relative to a very specific situation.

For example, a child has suddenly begun poking at other people. The poking behavior is increasing in frequency and has begun to interfere with the child's daily routines and interactions with others. The behavior specialist designs an ABC chart for the therapists and family to record data about the events prior to and following the poking.

The chart would include a space for the antecedent. The therapist makes a note briefly explaining what happened right before the behavior. The description of the antecedent must be observable. For example, the therapist would write, "TSS verbally prompted the child to keep her hands still." How you record information is a very important part of providing therapy. This data is used by the team and leads to changes in how sessions are conducted.

The chart would also include a space for a description of the behavior itself. Again, the description of the behavior must be measurable and observable. Instead of writing, "The child became agitated and poked the TSS," the therapist would write, "The child poked the TSS in the chest four times in less than one minute." This gives the team a clear understanding of the behavior and provides concrete data (in this case: *four times in less than one minute*) that can be compared to data collected after the therapist begins to implement different responses to the behavior.

Finally, the chart would include space to record a measurable consequence for the behavior. For example, the therapist would not write, "The child did not want to keep her hands still, so the TSS put her in time out." Instead the therapist writes, "The child was put in time out and resumed the activity with TSS after sixty seconds."

Consequences for the behavior do not always have to be negative. The therapist may choose to ignore the behavior and proceed as if nothing had happened. This planned ignoring is called **extinction**. The treatment team uses extinction to reduce the occurrences of some behaviors. This approach tends to yield very good results. I think of extinction as a bulldozer. My behavior bulldozes right over the child's behavior. Sometimes the child simply wants to see the response. If the child does not get any feedback for the behavior, it is less likely to reoccur.

Now, you might be wondering ....

9. What treatment program is used most frequently? **Page # 16**
12. What are autism & PDD? **Page # 21**
28. What is applied behavioral analysis? **Page # 42**
29. What is behavior? **Page # 44**
36. What are discrete trials? **Page # 54**
37. What are the phases of discrete trial drills? **Page # 56**
38. What is a drill? **Page # 58**
40. How do drills relate to applied behavioral analysis? **Page # 62**
50. What is the crisis plan? **Page # 78**
51. How do bubble sheets fit into the therapist's work? **Page # 80**
56. What is an incident report? **Page # 90**
57. What is a maintenance program? **Page # 92**
58. What is a Picture Exchange Communication System and how is it used? **Page # 93**
59. What is the program book? **Page # 94**
63. How does a therapist, 'shape,' behavior? **Page # 100**
68. After skills are mastered, how does a therapist generalize these to different settings? **Page # 107**

QUESTION 55
What is a token economy system?

A token economy system is a way to motivate children by establishing, "tokens," that are distributed and later exchanged for rewards to reinforce positive behavior. This system is practical and easy to use in a number of settings. A token economy system can take many forms, so it can easily be catered to fit the child's interests and likes. The system is tangible and visual and easy for many children to comprehend, and it helps the child learn cause-and-effect cycles.

The treatment team can work together to develop a token economy system by first selecting a tangible token. Common tokens include:

~ Stickers. These can be used effectively because they are appealing to many children and they are easy to manipulate. They also do not pose a choking hazard that other tokens do. Stickers are great for younger children.

~ Coins.

~ Marbles. These are wonderful to use for some children. I have worked with a number of children who love their marbles. They are interesting to many children because they are simply nice to look at. It is important to note that some of these items can pose a choking hazard. The family and the rest of the treatment team works together to determine which tokens are appropriate for each client.

~ Happy faces and stars are classic classroom token rewards that thrill some children.

~ Pictures of the child's favorite objects can be used as well. These tokens are great because they can be adhered to a token board with Velcro.

When it comes to a token system, the treatment team decides how the tokens will be used. If transitions are difficult, the child immediately gets a token each time he transitions from one activity to another without incident. The team also needs to decide how many tokens the child needs to earn before trading them in for the reward. For example, if the child earns four tokens, he gets a ten-minute break. When the token economy system is first introduced, the child is immediately given a reward once the first token is earned.

The family can carry the token economy system into the child's daily routines. A child can earn tokens during mealtime, bath time or nearly any daily activity. The family can determine when to use the token economy system. It is helpful to explain the steps to the system for the parents so they have a clear understanding of the process. Just as tokens are chosen according to the child's specific interests, reinforcers are chosen according to the child's interests. These subtle parts of therapy help the team to establish the right environment, where the child gets rewards that motivate them to participate and learn.

Now, you might be wondering ....

9. What is Wraparound? **Page # 16**
12. What are autism & PDD? **Page # 21**
28. What is applied behavioral analysis? **Page # 42**
29. What is behavior? **Page # 44**
38. What is a drill? **Page # 58**
40. How do drills relate to applied behavioral analysis? **Page # 62**
50. What is the crisis plan? **Page # 78**
51. How do bubble sheets fit into the therapist's work? **Page # 80**
56. What is an incident report? **Page # 90**
57. What is a maintenance program? **Page # 92**
58. What is a Picture Exchange Communication System and how is it used? **Page # 93**
59. What is the program book? **Page # 94**
63. How does a therapist, 'shape,' behavior? **Page # 100**
68. After skills are mastered, how does a therapist generalize these to different settings? **Page # 107**

Creating the therapeutic environment

In the same way that the crisis plan puts important controls into the therapeutic setting, establishing a token economy system helps to guide the sessions and give the child reference points for relating to others.

In a short term program such as Wraparound, where professionals go into the home, teaching the family ways to help their child is usually just as important as the work with the child. Helping the family to understand the benefits of something like a token economy system is a good way to help the family to begin creating a healthy, learning conducive, environment.

QUESTION 56
What is an incident report?

A therapist has to fill out an incident report whenever property is damaged or whenever someone is injured. A good rule of thumb is to fill out an incident report if you utilized any interventions included in the crisis plan. For example, a child has a tantrum and repeatedly hits his head against the table. The therapist moves the child to the middle of the room and removes any objects that are in his reach. This information is included in the report.

Just like all other documentation, the incident report only includes objective information about the episode. It is not necessary to include what you think the child was feeling. That is often evident in his actions. The report includes what happened during the occurrence, what interventions were used by the therapist and the time and location that the incident occurred. The report also includes how the incident concluded. For example, the child's parents and the therapist examined the child for any injury and found none, but the child was taken to the emergency room for examination.

An incident report should also be completed if the police get involved. For example, the child's mother is backing out of the driveway and hits the therapist's car. They exchange insurance information and the accident is reported to the police. In this case, an incident report is filled out even though the child is not directly involved with the accident.

Police and doctors do not have to be involved in all incident reports. It is a good idea to document occurrences that are unusual or may have ramifications in the future. For example, I fell up (yes, up) steps while leaving a school shift. I was embarrassed, but not hurt. I still completed an incident report in case the embarrassment wore off and the pain began. Another cautionary incident report is one that is filled out if property is damaged. The damage may be caused by the client or the staff. For example, the therapist leans against a counter and knocks a glass onto the floor, breaking it. The family may not be concerned with the minor incident, but it is good practice to fill out a report. "When in doubt, fill it out," as our secretary says.

It is also good practice to keep a blank incident report with you anytime you are working outside the office in the field. You may never need one, but it is best to be prepared. It is always good practice to keep blank copies of all forms that you will need.

Most therapists use a narrow three-ring binder to organize paperwork. The binders are convenient and easy to carry. They come in very handy during community and school settings. It makes it easy to turn to the appropriate form without going through piles of papers. This is especially handy when working in schools. This way, the therapist can quickly get a teacher's signature without disrupting the class. Being unobtrusive is part of the therapist's role in the school setting.

Now, you might be wondering ....

9. What treatment program is used most frequently? **Page # 16**
12. What are autism & PDD? **Page # 21**
28. What is applied behavioral analysis? **Page # 42**
29. What is behavior? **Page # 44**
36. What are discrete trials? **Page # 54**
38. What is a drill? **Page # 58**
40. How do drills relate to applied behavioral analysis? **Page # 62**
50. What is the crisis plan? **Page # 78**
57. What is a maintenance program? **Page # 92**
59. What is the program book? **Page # 94**
63. How does a therapist, 'shape,' behavior? **Page # 100**
68. After skills are mastered, how does a therapist generalize these to different settings? **Page # 107**

Asperger's Syndrome & Autism

Asperger's syndrome is a neurocognitive disorder that results in a number of problems for the afflicted child or adult. The truly interesting thing about Asperger's is that, while an afflicted individual may exhibit autistic-like behaviors, such as a lack of social skills or empathy, individuals with Asperger's tend to have incredibly heightened linguistic skills. Many autistic children are entirely non-verbal. Even where some communication skills are present, these are normally deficient compared to other children. By comparison, Asperger's children tend to seem precocious, highly intelligent and capable of complex reasoning and logic. This aspect of Asperger's is the reason why the condition remained somewhat mysterious for many years. Because the behaviors associated with Asperger's were so similar to autism, with the exception of linguistic skills, it was common for physicians to ponder exactly what caused the irratic behavior that occurs as a result of Asperger's.

QUESTION 57

What is a maintenance program?

A child will master many new skills and learn a lot of new information through therapy. In order to make sure that the child does not lose any of the skills, the treatment team has to make a conscious effort to reintroduce previously mastered skills into the therapy. Most clients who have been receiving services for awhile will have a maintenance book. The maintenance book contains drills and activities that the child has mastered. Even though the child probably uses those skills in general settings, it is a good idea to go over the mastered drills at least once each week.

If the child has mastered only a few drills, the maintenance drills may be in a section of the program book. If the child has mastered more than three drills, the treatment team will create a maintenance book containing mastered drills. The maintenance book may also include fine motor skills and gross motor skills as well as other program activities that address goals.

I have seen varied methods of collecting data on maintenance drills. Some maintenance books have a percentage graph and bubble sheets. A therapist approaches the mastered drills as he would approach others. The therapist simply records the date that the drill was reviewed. If the child does poorly on the drill, the therapist makes a note for the rest of the treatment team. If the child consistently does poorly on the maintenance drill, it will be reintroduced into the regular program.

It is not uncommon for a mastered drill to be reintroduced into the child's regular routine. The child may lose one or two targets, or he may lose the skill in its entirety. I worked with a child who suddenly did not respond to the command, "come sit." The child had previously mastered the command. The treatment team reintroduced the drill from the beginning. I would give the command, "come sit," and if he followed the command, I immediately rewarded him with a treat and told him to, "go play." We gradually had him sit for longer increments of time until he remastered the skill, requiring no prompts or rewards. Children with autism have a tendency to lose skills if they are not practiced, so it is important to keep up with maintenance and it is important to encourage the child to generalize mastered skills.

Now, you might be wondering ....

1. What is a therapist (TSS)? **Page # 6**
5. What is a behavioral specialist? **Page # 11**
42. What is a target? **Page # 66**
49. What is the treatment plan? **Page # 76**

What is a Picture Exchange Communication System and how is it used?

QUESTION 58

PECS is an anagram for Picture Exchange Communication System. PECS are simply pictures printed on two-inch by two-inch laminated cards. This communication system was developed in 1988 and it was first used at the Delaware Autistic Program. The therapist encourages the child to use pictures to access wants and needs. Within the treatment plan, the Picture Exchange Communication System is used to address communication and compliance goals. The cards are very useful because they give the child a visual prompt to help him understand spoken language.

It is important to start with an item or activity that motivates the child. There are six steps in using the PECS in relation to Applied Behavioral Analysis:

1. Encourage the child to exchange a picture for a desired object or activity. The goal of this step is to get the child to initiate communication without prompts.
2. Encourage the child to look for a picture and encourage the child to find someone to exchange the picture for the item or activity. The goal of this step is to get the child to actively communicate.
3. Encourage the child to choose the picture that represents the item or activity out of a number of other pictures. The goal of this step is to get the child to recognize that each picture represents a unique item or activity.
4. Encourage the child to recognize and use sentences to access the desired item or activity. The goal of this step is to get the child to use language to make requests.
5. Encourage the child to give an appropriate response to "What do you want?" The goal of this step is to help ease the child's frustration when trying to access wants and needs.
6. Encourage the child to respond to a variety of questions and encourage the child to make spontaneous statements. The goal of this step is to get the child to use functional language in a variety of settings.

The pictures may also be used to create a visual schedule to help the child understand what to expect during the session.

Now, you might be wondering ....

39. How do drills adhere to the treatment plan? **Page # 60**
40. How do drills relate to applied behavioral analysis? **Page # 62**
53. What is a visual treatment schedule? **Page # 84**
63. How does a therapist, 'shape,' behavior? **Page # 100**

QUESTION 59

What is the program book?

The program book is a large binder that is used in home therapy, containing drills and activities specifically developed for the case. Each drill and activity is placed in its own section of the program book. The drills and activities target specific skills and address goals outlined in the client's treatment plan. This is the most valuable tool for the team's home therapy sessions.

The program book is used by the therapist as a means of organizing the shift. It also contains data used to track the child's progress. Programs are altered according to the client's progress or lack of progress as it is recorded through this tool.

Because the programs are designed according to needs and goals outlined in the treatment plan, the treatment plan is kept in the program book. Many behavior specialists write a brief outline of needs, goals and interventions addressed in the treatment plan. This *cheat sheet* helps the therapists assigned to the case decide which interventions to use and what goals are being addressed.

The first thing found in a program book is a list of information relating to the client. This information helps substitute staff members and new staff members work with the child with little or no help.

The list includes:

1. Location of supplies used for therapy.
2. The client's preferred activities and rewards.
3. Miscellaneous information that is helpful in running a smooth shift.

Using information from the list, the therapist can quickly gather materials and choose drills and activities to engage the child.

The drills and activities correlate to goals cited in the treatment plan and are arranged in order. The staff uses a drill checklist to keep track of what drills and activities were completed during the previous shift. This helps to rotate the exercises each shift.

Skills include gross motor, fine motor and self help exercises. Each area has its own section in the program book with a list of activities that relate to the section. For example, jumping and arm circles fall under *gross motor*. Lacing and drawing fall under *fine motor*. Self help skills include anything from washing hands to putting on socks.

Skills vary from client to client according to need. Activities that address skills essentially address compliance and attention.

Now, you might be wondering ....

28. What is applied behavioral analysis? **Page # 42**
40. How do drills relate to applied behavioral analysis? **Page # 62**
41. What is a discrete stimulus or SD? **Page # 64**
49. What is the treatment plan? **Page # 76**
50. What is the crisis plan? **Page # 78**
51. How do bubble sheets fit into the therapist's work? **Page # 80**
56. What is an incident report? **Page # 90**
57. What is a maintenance program? **Page # 92**

Psychologists of note

Though he is known world wide as a major contributor to the body of knowledge associated with developmental psychology, Dr. Reuven Feuerstein is not yet a common name in the United States. He is best known for his assertions regarding intelligence and the possibility that an individual can, through specific interventions, develop greater levels of intelligence and functioning.

Though there are still questions regarding its effectiveness, Dr. Reuven Feuerstein's, 'Instrumental Enrichment (IE),' program is a vast series of interventions that may be used by everyone from the mentally challenged to the gifted to (*supposedly*) help shape cognitive structure in such a way that it will help them to enhance development.

A good place to learn about Dr. Feuerstein's programs and other similar advancements is at: **www.newhorizons.org**. Check it out!

THERAPEUTIC ACTIVITIES & STRATEGIES

Your Questions Answered on...

60. What are some activities that help special needs children with fine and gross motor faculties? **Page # 97**

61. What are some examples of engaging activities? **Page # 98**

62. How is 'desensitizing,' used in therapy with sensory issues? **Page #99**

63. How does a therapist, 'shape,' behavior? **Page # 100**

64. How are social stories used in shaping? **Page # 102**

65. What does a typical social story look like? **Page # 104**

66. How are distractors used in therapy? **Page # 105**

67. What is superstitous learning? **Page # 106**

68. After skills are mastered, how does a therapist generalize these to different settings? **Page # 107**

69. What activities help a child develop cognitive processes? **Page # 108**

70. What are some strategies for working with families? **Page # 110**

71. What strategies are used to engage autistic children in activities? **Page # 111**

72. What are some strategies for teaching replacement behaviors? **Page # 113**

73. What strategies are used for teaching idioms? **Page # 115**

74. What strategies are used to motivate autistic children? **Page # 117**

75. What strategies are used to reduce self-stimulatory behaviors? **Page # 118**

76. What strategies are used to reduce verbal perseveration? **Page # 119**

77. What are some strategies to help an autistic child integrate sensory information? **Page # 121**

What are some activities that help autistic children with fine and gross motor faculties?

QUESTION 60

Gross motor activities involve large body movements, like walking. Fine motor activities involve smaller movements, like writing. The child's program book will usually contain a gross motor and a fine motor checklist. Some gross motor and fine motor skills are specifically used to help the child develop coordination that they commonly lack due to insufficient body awareness or sensory issues.

Common gross motor activities include walking, stomping and jumping. Walking is often taken for granted, but it is a complex activity for many individuals. A common problem for autistic children is the tendancy to walk on their toes. The term used is, "toe-walking." If the child persists in doing this, his tendons and ligaments may not develop properly. A therapist may engage the child in gross motor activities that involve pressing his heels into the floor. Stomping and jumping are often rewarding for the child. I like to incorporate songs into these kinds of gross motor activities. "If You're Happy and You Know It," is a great song to facilitate a number of gross motor skills for a child motivated by music. You can also use the song to address attention and auditory processing skills. The child responds to receptive commands throughout the song. For example, "if you're happy and you know it, stomp your feet." The child processes the command, "stomp your feet." If the child can not follow receptive commands, the therapist can use the song for nonverbal imitation simply by stomping while singing, "stomp your feet."

Fine motor activities involve smaller movements mostly involving the hands. Common fine motor activities include coloring, drawing and buttoning. The child's program book will usually include a checklist of fine motor activity ideas to use throughout the shift. I have found that most of the children I work with struggle with fine motor activities, but these skills are essential for taking part in school and self-help skills. These activities address compliance goals and attention goals because they are often challenging. They address nonverbal imitation if the therapist serves as a model for the activity.

Fine motor and gross motor activities and sensory integration also provide structured sensory outlets. This helps the child work through sensory problems.

Now, you might be wondering ....

15. How do autistic children suffer from body awareness deficiencies? **Page # 26**
16. What sensory issues affect autistic & PDD children? **Page # 27**

QUESTION 61

What are some examples of engaging activities?

I like to incorporate the child's drills into play, but it is important to keep the drills themselves structured and consistent. While the play activities spark the child's interests, we have to be careful not to confuse work with play. The goal of these activities is to get the child to interact with you, which leads to the development of social skills.

One of my favorite engaging activities is *Row-Row-Row Your Boat*. I sit facing the child and take his hands in mine. I begin the song very slowly, pulling back-and-forth as if we are rowing. I then pretend that the child is getting heavier with each pull, until I fall forward and finally lean back pretending that he is just too heavy for me to pull anymore, but then I muster the strength to pull him up. This activity has yielded great results and I have even used it as a tool for teaching a child to string words together using sign language.

The Row-Row-Row Your Boat exercise addresses the proprioceptive system, the vestibular system as well as visual, auditory and tactile senses. You can also encourage the child to make eye contact by stopping the activity until he looks at you. Once the child makes eye contact, continue the activity.

Peek-a-boo is a great game if it is done with the right child. I have played peek-a-boo with children who just would not look for me. It is important to have a good idea of where the child is developmentally. Many children are out-of-sight-out-of-mind. I use a blanket for the peek-a-boo game and alter the activity according to the child's reaction. Some children enjoy the surprise of you popping out from behind the blanket, others may like to pull the blanket down on their own. You can also put the blanket over the child's head and say, "where's ____?" Then pull the blanket down and tickle or praise the child.

If you are the theatrical type, use your dramatic flair. Pretend that your mouth is stuck shut and motion for the child to unzip it. Play yucky/yummy with pretend food. Use pictures of foods to prompt the child. If you are working on labeling animals and foods, you can reinforce the child's learning by having the child match the food to the animal, then act like the animal eating the food. I once did this for a child who loved it so much when I acted like a monkey eating a banana, that the child would initiate his Receptive Animals drill by getting the materials out and setting them at his workstation.

Now, you might be wondering ....

16. What sensory issues affect autistic & PDD children? **Page # 27**
17. What are tactile, vestibular and proprioceptive systems? **Page # 28**

How is 'desensitizing,' used in therapy with sensory issues?

QUESTION 62

Children diagnosed within the autism spectrum of disorders often have many sensory issues that make everyday activities intolerable. The child may be hypersensitive to sound or touch. Some children can not tolerate certain textures in their mouths. Eating and brushing teeth can be very challenging for these children. Intolerance to textures in the mouth is a tactile intolerance. Sensory issues can involve any of the senses, but auditory and tactile difficulties tend to be most common.

One child I worked with could not stand to have her hair brushed. The behavior specialist introduced a method of desensitizing the child to the sensation of having her hair brushed. The treatment team began desensitizing by first using a silky fabric. We ran the fabric over the child's skin. We used the fabric during play activities, hiding behind it during a game of peek-a-boo. Gradually, we put the fabric on the child's head for increasingly longer periods of time.

Once the child tolerated having the fabric on her head, we used a hat in the same way. The child handled the hat. We played with the hat and gradually the child wore the hat. She was praised and rewarded for tolerating the sensation of wearing the fabric and she was praised and rewarded for wearing the hat.

After she tolerated wearing a hat, we began using our hands in small steps. We used our hands as puppets during play and as peek-a-boo shields. We would press lightly on her head with our hands and gradually stroke her head with our hands, praising and rewarding every tolerant step of the way.

Therapy reached a point where the child could tolerate having her hair stroked for over a minute. The next step was to introduce the brush. We began with a very soft brush and let the child play with the brush. We ran the brush over her skin and encouraged her to imitate. We would brush our own hair and prompt her to brush our hair as well.

The child eventually began brushing other people's hair and her doll's hair. She even brushed her own hair, but she still whined when someone else brushed her hair. Eventually, the child tolerated having her hair brushed in a number of settings, even a playground, but as you can see, it took a number of steps and many hours of therapy.

Now, you might be wondering ....

16. What sensory issues affect autistic & PDD children? **Page # 27**
17. What are tactile, vestibular and proprioceptive systems? **Page # 28**
18. How do self-stimulatory behaviors involve the senses? **Page # 29**

QUESTION 63
How does a therapist, 'shape,' behavior?

Shaping is a step-by-step process that builds on the child's current skills leading to a desired behavior. When a therapist is shaping a behavior, she reinforces skills that gradually lead to a desired behavior. This process does not happen over night, but it is effective because it works with a child's strengths to help them develop.

1. The target behavior has to be defined. What is it that we want the child to do? How do we want the child to behave?

2. Determine what skills the child exhibits that are approximations of the behavior. An approximation is any behavior that resembles the target behavior. The team uses approximations to inch the child closer to the target.

3. Reward approximations to the behavior. Sometimes the child takes a step forward and exhibits a behavior closer to the target behavior. Sometimes the child takes a step backwards. Consistently reward approximate behavior that is closer to the target, but if the child regresses, go back to rewarding the previous approximation.

4. Prompt the child to use a new approximation of the target behavior that takes him one step closer. The improvement that you prompt needs to be slight. It is best to take very small steps in the shaping process.

5. Collect data on the results. Clear, objective, data can help determine if the team is moving in the right direction. The team may need to take a step back in the approach or they may need to increase their expectations and hasten the progress of therapy.

Applied Behavior Analysis shapes a child's behavior by breaking down tasks into small steps. The target behaviors involve *compliance, attention, communication* and *social skills*. The child is rewarded for appropriate responses and motivated to repeat the desired behavior. Once a step is mastered, the child is introduced to the next step and the process continues.

Consider an example where the target behavior is for the child to wait for at least three minutes. The behavior specialist designs a *Wait* drill. The first step is to give the child the verbal cue, "wait," and prompt the child to wait for three seconds. The child is immediately rewarded and praised for waiting. Many times a therapist will repeat the original command while praising. "Good job waiting!" or, "That's waiting!" are a couple of options. Once the child has consistently demonstrated that he can wait for three seconds, the increments of time increase to five seconds. The therapist then extends the time to ten seconds, fifteen seconds, and so on until the child waits for three minutes without prompts and without rewards.

Now, you might be wondering ....

1. What is a therapist (TSS)? **Page # 6**
5. What is a behavioral specialist? **Page # 11**
9. What treatment program is used most frequently? **Page # 16**
28. What is applied behavioral analysis? **Page # 42**
29. What is behavior? **Page # 44**
35. How are positive and negative reinforcement used in therapy? **Page # 53**
36. What are discrete trials? **Page # 54**
37. What are the phases of discrete trial drills? **Page # 56**
38. What is a drill? **Page # 58**
39. How do drills adhere to the treatment plan? **Page # 60**
40. How do drills relate to applied behavioral analysis? **Page # 62**
49. What is the treatment plan? **Page # 76**
100. I think I want to work with special needs children, where should I start? **Page # 159**

Early autism theories

Early on in the study of autism, psychoanalysts theorized that autism was the result of cold, emotionally distant, mothers, whose behavior made it impossible for the child to create the bonds necessary for normal development. These mothers were termed, 'refrigerator mothers.'

In 1964, Bernard Rimland, a psychologist with an autistic son, published a book that directly countered the 'refrigerator mother,' explanation for autism.

Working as a part of a treatment team, or in any role that brings you in contact with the families of special needs children, it is important to be sensitive to family members. Many blame themselves for their child's condition. Some believe that other's hold them responsible. The family is an important part of the team and every professional that they come into contact with much work hard to reassure them.

QUESTION 64: How are social stories used in shaping?

Social stories were developed by an autism consultant named Carol Gray. The social stories are used to help autistic children navigate through social situations by helping the child see things from another person's point of view. The stories are designed in a systematic structure that eases the child through the perception process one step at a time. They serve as a model for appropriate behavior in various social situations. The stories help the child recognize social cues that may tell the child how another person perceives the situation.

There are four steps to the social stories:

1. Descriptive step - The social stories begin with a description of the setting and social situation. The descriptive sentences include the activity, the people involved and what the people do in the social setting.

2. Directive step - The directive step describes what the child should do in the social situation. The directive step includes sentences that are clear and concise. The child is given a step-by-step instruction on how to behave in the situation. The directive step should include a number of alternatives for the child to use so the child does not become rigid in his response.

3. Perspective step - The perspective step includes descriptions of how other people experience the social situation. The step uses sentences to describe other people's reactions and prompts the child to see things from different points of view.

4. Control step - The control step includes sentences that the therapist develops with the child after the social story's first three steps are completed. The control step helps the child remember and comprehend the story.

Carol Grey also developed a ratio of sentences in each step. For every directive or control sentence in the steps, there should be between two and five descriptive or perspective sentences. The child needs to visualize the social situation and will require more description about the situation and the other people's responses. The child's directive and control responses are gradually faded as the child becomes familiar with the social cues. The descriptive and perspective steps set up the scenario and the directive and control steps tell the child how to respond to the scenario.

Social stories address the child's individual needs and are developed to help a child through specific social situations. The child's treatment team may identify a specific social situation that is challenging for the child (such as going from a classroom to a bus). The behavior specialist uses the steps in the social story format to create a social story specific to the child's needs. Typical social stories address home, school and community situations including everything from having visitors over to waiting in line in the mall.

Now, you might be wondering ....

1. What is a therapist (TSS)? **Page # 6**
5. What is a behavioral specialist? **Page # 11**
9. What treatment program is used most frequently? **Page # 16**
28. What is applied behavioral analysis? **Page # 42**
29. What is behavior? **Page # 44**
35. How are positive and negative reinforcement used in therapy? **Page # 53**
36. What are discrete trials? **Page # 54**
63. How does a therapist, 'shape,' behavior? **Page # 100**
65. What does a typical social story look like? **Page # 104**

Getting acquainted with anxiety

Professionals who spend their time working with special needs children tend to have one common attribute: the ability to handle stress. Whether you are working with a child moving through the juvenile court system, an individual with autism in a Wraparound program or an Asperger's afflicted child in a residential facility, the one thing that will remain constant is that these children will exhibit behaviors that are in some way connected to reducing their own anxiety levels - and those behaviors are at times going to be directed at you. It is important to remember that the child's anxiety results from their own inability to understand and come to terms with their environment.

If you decide to pursue a career spent working with special needs children, expect to face high stress situations. The ability to cope with these types of situations is one of the most important skills employed in this profession.

Question 65

What does a typical social story look like?

Although each social story is created specifically for the child's social needs, the stories follow a specific format and they take the child through a step-by-step scripting process that helps regulate behavior in social settings. First, the treatment team identifies a problem and determines that a social story is the best approach to addressing it. The behavior specialist develops a script including sentences in each of the four steps of the social story format.

Here is an example of a social story for a child who has difficulty waiting for his bus. The child would be taught to say these phrases to himself as he goes through the steps from leaving the classroom to waiting for the bus:

1. Descriptive step - The bell rings. The school day is over. The children wait in their seats. The teacher tells the children when their bus is ready to take them home. The teacher tells the children to get in line. The children get in line and walk to their bus. They sit in their seats on the bus. The bus takes the children home.

2. Directive step - I sit quietly in my seat. When the teacher tells me to, I walk with the other children who ride on my bus. I keep my hands to myself and I walk slowly. I safely get on the bus and sit still in my seat.

3. Perspective step - The teacher is happy to see me sitting quietly in my seat. The children are excited to go home. The teacher is proud of me when I get in line when she tells me to. The children are happy when we all walk slowly and safely to our buses. The bus driver is happy when I sit quietly in my seat on the bus.

4. Control step - I know that the school day is over when the bell rings. I can wait quietly for the teacher to tell me it is time to go. The bus will not leave without me.

The social story can be altered according to the child's needs. In the example above, the child has difficulty waiting. Instead of using the social story to tell the child what he shouldn't do, the therapist uses the story to tell the child what he should do.

Now, you might be wondering ....

63. How does a therapist, 'shape,' behavior? **Page # 100**
64. How are social stories used in shaping? **Page # 102**

How are distractors used in therapy?

QUESTION 66

A distracter is anything that a therapist uses to distract the child from the target in a drill. Usually drills that use letters, shapes or objects, follow the same format. Each drill begins with the child working with the target in isolation. Once the target is mastered in isolation, the therapist moves the target into random rotation. Some children have difficulty making the jump from isolation to random rotation. If a child consistently demonstrates confusion once the target is rotated with other targets, the behavior specialist may introduce another step. This step involves using a *distractor*.

For example, a child manages to master two colors in isolation. However, once the colors are randomly rotated, the child confuses them. The behavior specialist can introduce distractors to help the child become more familiar with the colors before moving on. Using a distractor is not the usual approach for discrete trial drills, but it often yields positive results.

The therapist presents the color blue in isolation in a receptive colors drill. There is nothing on the workstation except the target color blue. After the child demonstrates that he can consistently touch the color blue when given the SD, "touch blue," the therapist introduces a distractor. The distractor is placed next to the color blue and the therapist gives the SD, "touch blue." The child has to discriminate between the target color and the distractor in order to touch the target.

I have seen distractors used a couple of different ways. In most cases, the distractor is very different from the target. If the target is the color blue a good distractor is a fire truck. For some cases, it is very important to keep the distractor distinct so the child can follow through. This also helps the drill maintain a format that is close to a traditional drill. Using a distractor that is vastly different from the target is closer to isolation than using a distractor that is similar to the target.

Usually, distractors are not necessary, but they can help the child become familiar with the targets before the child has to discriminate between them.

Now, you might be wondering ....

38. What is a drill? **Page # 58**
39. How do drills adhere to the treatment plan? **Page # 60**
40. How do drills relate to applied behavioral analysis? **Page # 62**
41. What is a discrete stimulus or SD? **Page # 64**
42. What is a target? **Page # 66**
43. How is a target introduced? **Page # 67**
44. What if a child can not master a target? **Page # 68**

QUESTION 67

What is superstitous learning?

B.F. Skinner, one of the strongest advocates for Behaviorism, is known widely for a group of experients that demonstrated superstitious learning. One experiment involved giving pigeons food every few seconds, no matter how they behaved. After awhile, the pigeons began repeating the last movement they made before the food was released. This is an example of superstitious learning. Another example would be a baseball player wearing a lucky undershirt beneath his uniform because he was wearing the undershirt the last time his team won a game. There is no correlation between the pigeon's actions and the food, as there is no correlation between the undershirt and winning the game. This behavior is said to have been learned *superstitously*.

This same situation takes place during therapy. For example, the therapist instructs the child to look at her. The child says, "more," in response. Later, the therapist prompts the child to say, "I want," and the child says, "more," again. The child is simply repeating the last response she remembers to have resulted in a reward. The child associated saying, "more," with getting treats, being allowed to use a swing set or any other desired reward.

I have seen a number of children go through an entire repertoire of skills hoping to hit the one that yields the desired result. When you consider how many targets and types of drills that you go through in a few hours, this type of response could involve the child doing everything from clapping to looking for specific toys to signing certain words. This is one of the reasons that drills are kept simple and the therapist works to keep instructions clear and to quickly redirect incorrect responses. Otherwise the child will focus on going through a series of actions or the child will focus on using all the words she knows in order to gain reinforcement.

Now, you might be wondering ....

36. What are discrete trials? **Page # 54**
40. How do drills relate to applied behavioral analysis? **Page # 62**
41. What is a discrete stimulus or SD? **Page # 64**
42. What is a target? **Page # 66**
63. How does a therapist, 'shape,' behavior? **Page # 100**

After skills are mastered, how does a therapist generalize these to different settings?

QUESTION 68

Generalizing skills is when the therapist or other members of the team take a skill that the child has learned and begins having the child use this in other settings. The setting can be another room in the home, in the community or even in a different part of the therapy room. The child may need a little prompting at first to segue into different settings.

Let's say that a child has mastered the letters in the alphabet in the Receptive Letters drill. The therapist may use an alphabet puzzle to generalize letters. She would do this by placing two or three pieces of the letter puzzle in front of the child and prompt him to pick a specific letter. The child demonstrates that he recognizes the letter by choosing the appropriate letter. After this, the child may be prompted to touch various letters in different settings, such as magnetic letters on the refrigerator or letters and images on a sign in the park.

Another drill that can be used in a number of settings is the, "come sit," drill. This is a fundamental skill that the child has to learn early on in therapy in order to be considered, "table ready." After the child learns the skill, the treatment team can prompt the child to sit on the floor, bed, couch and chair, moving it into a generalized setting.

The importance of 'generalized skills?' - There's not much use in providing therapy for a special needs child if they're never going to be able to use the skills they have learned outside of therapy. For this reason, the work done with a child to help generalize skills is very important. Initially, the therapist will be the one helping the child to apply skills in various settings, but since many programs are temporary, the ongoing generalizing activities will fall on the family, teachers and other people that work with the child after these treatments have ended. The therapist and behavior specialist both work with the family to help them understand the proper ways to work with the child to get them to apply these new skills in many environments.

Now, you might be wondering ....

9. What treatment program is used most frequently? **Page # 16**
78. What goals do therapists address during a visit to a playground? **Page # 124**
79. How are sensory needs addressed during a trip to the playground? **Page # 126**
80. What is the therapist's role in the classroom? **Page # 128**
81. What are some general rules the therapist follows in the classroom? **Page # 130**
82. How is the treatment plan addressed in community settings? **Page # 132**

QUESTION 69
What activities help a child develop cognitive processes?

Many play activities can help a child who has executive function deficits to develop cognitive processes that may be lacking. This is the reason that many treatment plans incorporate games and other play activities into therapy. When the behaviorist works to develop this plan, they first determine which cognitive process needs to be addressed. This is done either by using previously gathered information on the child or through observations made throughout the course of therapy.

The following are specific cognitive processes, behaviors exhibited when the child has issues with this process and suggestions for activities:

1. Working memory

1. Difficulty following rules to multi-step games
2. Difficulty remembering the goal of a task
3. Forgets important steps in a task
4. Difficulty sequencing steps in a task

Good play activities to engage a child who demonstrates these characteristics include tic-tac-toe, Guess Who and checkers. The therapist may include other family members in a game of telephone, in which the same story is whispered from one person to another. The person who hears the story repeats it to the next person. The goal is to keep the story in working memory as accurately as possible so the last person tells the same story as the first.

2. Cognitive flexibility

1. Difficulty adapting to new situations
2. Difficulty showing empathy
3. Difficulty seeing another person's point of view
4. Difficulty seeing the impact his behavior has on others
5. Difficulty considering different responses

Reciprocal games like tic-tac-toe and checkers are good for developing cognitive flexibility because the child's next move relies on the other player's move. Charades helps the child develop an understanding of how other people perceive his actions. The child has to adapt his actions according to the other people's responses.

3. Organizing and planning

1. Difficulty initiating activities

2. Difficulty playing alone
3. Difficulty anticipating consequences
4. Repetitive questions about upcoming activities

Sequencing games are effective in developing organizing and planning processes. The therapist can help a child pack for a play camping trip. The child has to find things he will need while camping, map a destination and sequence events of the trip.

4. Problem Solving

1. Difficulty seeing more than one solution
2. Difficulty using clues
3. Difficulty using advice
4. Difficulty understanding abstract problems

Any game that involves strategy is effective in helping a child develop problem solving skills. Tic-tac-toe and checkers are examples, but nearly every board game requires some problem-solving skills.

5. Cognitive inhibition

1. Difficulty waiting for instructions before beginning activities
2. Difficulty considering consequences for actions
3. Difficulty taking time on task
4. Difficulty controlling emotion

Duck-duck-goose is a classic game that helps develop cognitive inhibition skills. The child has to wait and listen before acting. Simon Says also requires the child to wait and listen before acting.

Now, you might be wondering ....

71. What strategies are used to engage autistic children in activities? **Page # 111**
72. What are some strategies for teaching replacement behaviors? **Page # 113**
73. What strategies are used for teaching idioms? **Page # 115**
74. What strategies are used to motivate autistic children? **Page # 117**
75. What strategies are used to reduce self-stimulatory behaviors? **Page # 118**
76. What strategies are used to reduce verbal perseveration? **Page # 119**
77. What are some strategies to help an autistic child integrate sensory information? **Page # 121**

QUESTION 70: What are some strategies for working with families?

Therapists devote a great deal of time into trying to help autistic children develop empathy for other people. It is necessary for the therapist to also be empathetic for the families with whom they work. Wraparound and other services that involve bringing therapy to the client are invasive in nature. The families who receive services have a lot of people coming in and out of their homes. They have appointments to keep, careers to maintain and some have other children to care for as well.

Throughout therapy, the child is the client. The therapist works together with the family as a team, along the following dynamics:

1. **The parents are the team leaders** - A good therapist empowers them through communication. Letting the parents know that the child is starting to use sign language is a nice start. Showing the parents how to sign and encouraging them to prompt the child to use the sign as much as possible clearly communicates what the child is learning in therapy.
2. **The therapist is a model** - Demonstrating effective strategies is a great way to help parents get involved with the child's therapy.
3. **Keep it positive** - There's a bit of a public relations side to the therapist's job. They need to sandwich the child's struggles in between the child's strengths. No parent likes to hear that their child had a bad day. A good therapist points out that progress does not happen over night.
4. **Therapists are always asking for the parent's input** - The therapist not only carries out the treatment plan, but they act as a communicator, expressing parent's concerns to the behavior specialist and other team members.
5. **Therapists must maintain their professional distance** - Therapy takes time, both for the children and their families. It's best to hold back on advice and just let everyone learn through the process.
6. **Don't take things personally** - Families aren't always thrilled to have a therapist in their home. Expect at least a little resentment and the occassional cold shoulder.
7. **The therapist needs to connect with the client.** Even though a therapist needs to maintain their professionalism, this career involves personal interaction involving a great deal of communication (or at least attempts at communication). To really provide successful treatment, a therapist needs to make a connection with the client.

Now, you might be wondering ....

7. What types of conflicts arise within a treatment team? **Page # 13**
8. What are the benefits in working with special needs children? **Page # 15**
9. What treatment program is used most frequently? **Page # 16**

What strategies are used to engage autistic children in activities?

QUESTION 71

In many cases, play skills are considered a goal for treatment. Even if play is not formally listed as a goal in the treatment plan, play activities are still very valuable during a shift and help to engage the client. Each case is different and strategies that work for one child may not work for another. It depends on how the child takes in sensory information.

Tickles may make one child giggle and make eye contact, but tickles may make another child recoil. The therapist decides what approaches to take through close observation. For example, if a child is burrowing into the cushions on the couch, the therapist would know to use activities that address proprioceptive needs. If the child is rocking back-and-forth, activities that involve vestibular movement would be beneficial.

Activities that play on the child's needs and interests are usually the most engaging. The treatment plan is where the therapist can find useful information about the client with regards to capturing their interest. The behavior specialist normally includes the child's interests in the strengths section of the treatment plan. It also helps to ask the child's family members about interests the child may have.

Once the therapist discovers a few activities that interest the child, they should tailor them. Voice inflection, pauses and other affectations help to increase interest for the child, while also giving the child cues for when they should provide responses. Using fun activities, the therapist can keep the session moving towards specific goals.

Play activities include sensory integration as well. A therapist can address the child's sensory needs while developing a relationship with him. Sensory integration activities help the child calm and organize his behavior, focus on tasks and follow through with directions. Play activities are great motivators, too. Including play on a child's schedule is a good way to get them to complete a task.

There are a lot of activities to engage a child. The key is to find out what interests the child. The child may love a cartoon character, a nursery rhyme or a song. Any of these can be used as tools to gain the child's attention, communication and compliance.

Now, you might be wondering ....

1. What is a therapist (TSS)? **Page # 6**
16. What sensory issues affect autistic & PDD children? **Page # 27**
17. What are tactile, vestibular and proprioceptive systems? **Page # 28**

Knowing the lingo

Throughout this guide you've probably come across some lingo that you never experienced before. Covering everything from *ABC charts* to *functions of behavior*, there is a wide array of language used in careers related to working with special needs children that you're not going to hear outside of this field. All the way back at the beginning of this guide, many of the questions address how different professionals with varying roles work together to meet a specific goal. This is only accomplished so long as they can communicate effectively and express themselves in terms that everyone understands. Throughout the development of this guide, one of the goals was to give the reader a vast lexicon of the many specialized words used by professionals who work with special needs children. A good way to prepare yourself for your career is to pay special attention to any words you do not know. Developing a great professional vocabulary is not only necessary for your career, but when it comes time to get that job, use of words specific to a field is the easiest way to show interviewers that you know your stuff and can easily take part in a team environment where communication is key.

What are some strategies for teaching replacement behaviors?

QUESTION 72

Just as a therapist teaches a child replacement behaviors for their self-stimulatory behaviors, they also use replacement behaviors for negative and non-negotiable behaviors. In order to choose a replacement behavior, the treatment team needs to know the function of the original behavior. If the replacement does not satisfy the same function as the original behavior it simply won't work.

First, the treatment team has to determine the target behavior they want to change. The therapists and family members will record information about the target behavior on an ABC chart. The chart includes space to describe the antecedent and consequence of the target behavior. Using this information, the behavior specialist determines which replacement behavior to use and which interventions the team will use to replace the child's behavior. Following the behavior specialist's plan, the team begins to intervene on the target behavior.

Let's look at an example. A child begins stomping her feet, crying and pointing at the refrigerator everyday at a specific time. The team records that the *antecedent to the behavior* is the end of her break time. Her break ends at 11:30am. The *consequences for the behavior* vary according to who is home with her. Her grandmother asks her what she wants and opens the refrigerator. Her mother tells her it's not lunchtime yet and leads her to the therapy room and her father gives her a snack to take back to the room.

The therapists assigned to the case take objective data on the behavior, recording it on the ABC chart. Note that the team members do not tell the family members what they should be doing. The therapist just records what is occurring without making judgments or giving advice. The team has to work as a unit to find the function of the behavior in order to address it.

The function of this behavior is not as obvious as it appears. Only after reviewing the common antecedent can you really get a good idea of what the child uses this behavior to achieve. It would seem that the child is hungry and trying to communicate this, but if the child only indicates that she wants something to eat when she is directed to go back to the therapy room, chances are that she is using this behavior to keep from transitioning back into therapy after break. The behavior specialist may decide that the replacement behavior needs to address the way that the child is using the action of going into the kitchen to delay therapy. This delay can be taken as the child's way of communicating their desire to not proceed with therapy. A good replacement behavior would be having the child use pictures or signs to communicate wants and needs.

In this case, the treatment team would consistently prompt the child to exchange a picture representing eating before the end of the break. The team may also prompt her to sign, "eat," as well.

The function of the behavior will soon be apparent by how the child responds to the new intervention. If the child does not take the snack and repeats the behavior once the therapist directs her to go to the therapy room, the function of the behavior is avoidance and the team adjusts interventions accordingly. If the child exchanges the picture for a snack, then the behavior is the result of hunger. Either way, the team has uncovered the true motivation for the behavior and con progress from this knowledge.

It's important to note that the therapist does not offer advice to the family or even try to address these behaviors on-the-spot. Wraparound is a team effort that follows very strict procedures. If you decide to build a career around working with special needs children, you'll find that the approach is very scientific. Therapy is an on-going process that involves examining behaviors and addressing them with planned interventions.

Now, you might be wondering ....

54. What is an ABC chart? **Page # 86**
68. After skills are mastered, how does a therapist generalize these to different settings? **Page # 107**
69. What activities help a child develop cognitive processes? **Page # 108**
70. What are some strategies for working with families? **Page # 110**
71. What strategies are used to engage autistic children in activities? **Page # 111**
73. What strategies are used for teaching idioms? **Page # 115**

The frequency of autism

There is some debate on the number of people suffering from autism within the population. According to the The United States Centers for Disease Control (CDC), an estimated 1 out of every 500 to 1 out of every 166 births may be diagnosed with a disorder within the autism spectrum. The National Institute of Mental Health (NIMH) has provided a much different estimate, claiming that the conservative view would be as many 1 in 1000 births that may be diagnosed with an autism spectrum disorder. Either of these numbers shows a significant increase in the number of children diagnosed with a disorder over the last four decades.

What strategies are used for teaching idioms?

QUESTION 73

Idioms are difficult for an autistic child to understand. They understand language intellectually, taking the words at face value. The use of idiomatic language creates confusion because terms do not maintain their literal meaning.

High-functioning children who receive therapy often have a drill in their program that addresses figurative language, like idioms. The drills are related to communication and social goals. The strategies a behavior specialist would develop include:

1. Rote memorization.

Rote memorization is the lowest form of cognitive learning. It is a good starting point for addressing issues like figurative language. The child simply memorizes what the figure of speech means or what it correlates to.

2. Multiple choices.

The child is given a scenario and the therapist asks the child what idiom goes with the situation. For example, the scenario is: "Your mom tells you that she is giving your sister a surprise party. She doesn't want your sister to find out so she tells you to:"
a. Keep it under your hat.
b. Stop pulling my leg.
c. Let the cat out of the bag.

3. Fill-in the blank.

The child is given a scenario and the therapist asks the child to use an idiom that fits the scenario. The child must learn a number of idioms in order for this drill to be used. For example, the therapist uses the scenario, "The teacher caught Molly cheating on the test. The teacher calls Molly's mother to tell her. When Molly gets home she knows that she is in trouble. Her mother says _____." The child completes the phrase with an idiom like, "You're in hot water," or, "You're in the dog house."

There are a number of other ways to address idioms in a child's program. Behavior specialists develop many creative ways to help the child learn new skills and the intricacies of language. Each program is catered to the child according to his strengths and according to his needs. A child whose program includes drills like idioms is normally high-functioning, with decent communication skills and a need to acquire social language. A child who functions on this level may also show deficits in executive functioning.

Now, you might be wondering ....

68. After skills are mastered, how does a therapist generalize these to different settings? **Page # 107**
69. What activities help a child develop cognitive processes? **Page # 108**
70. What are some strategies for working with families? **Page # 110**
71. What strategies are used to engage autistic children in activities? **Page # 111**
72. What are some strategies for teaching replacement behaviors? **Page # 113**
74. What strategies are used to motivate autistic children? **Page # 117**
75. What strategies are used to reduce self-stimulatory behaviors? **Page # 118**
76. What strategies are used to reduce verbal perseveration? **Page # 119**
77. What are some strategies to help an autistic child integrate sensory information? **Page # 121**

Profiles: Eugene Bleuler

Eugene Bleuler is attributed as having been the first to use the word, 'autism,' in the English language. A Swiss psychiatrist, Bleuler used the word in an article he wrote for the *American Journal of Insanity*.

Originally, autism was used to describe a schizophrenic's trouble with relating to others. The word is derived from the Greek word for self, 'autos.'

It was not until 1943, that Dr. Leo Kanner, working at Johns Hopkins Hospital, establish autism as a classification for a lack of interest that some children had for other people. His research, along with thousands of hours of research since, have helped to develop our understanding of the disorder to the present day.

What strategies are used to motivate autistic children?

QUESTION 74

Self-stimulatory behaviors and sensory integration activities naturally motivate children to act. A therapist can use this to motivate an autistic child to follow directions, stay on task, communicate and relate to others. The activities can also be used to address fine motor and gross motor skills required for the child to navigate through everyday situations.

For example, a child who wants to tap items repeatedly can be prompted to bang on a drum. Banging on the drum is an activity that includes the child's auditory, visual and tactile senses. The therapist could involve nonverbal imitation (NVI) by encouraging the child to imitate the therapist's rhythm. This also works on the child's attention because the child has to focus on the therapist's actions. It addresses compliance because the child needs to follow directions to continue the activity. The therapist could prompt the child to say or sign, "more," to communicate that he would like to continue.

I worked with a team that used a child's self-stimulatory behavior as a tool that facilitated communication. In this case, the child was fascinated by letters. He often spelled words repeatedly. He liked to match letters and just look at letters. Even though letters seem like magnificent items to use in self-stimulatory behaviors, they can be problematic. The problem with this stim is that he was spelling words instead of saying them. He still was not communicating appropriately. However, when the team worked together to encourage him to say each word after spelling, he began slowly to just use the words rather than spelling. This was successful because the entire team worked as a unit. His parents encouraged him to use words in all settings and therapy was consistent. Part of the reason that the transition was successful also lies in the fact that, through therapy, the child simply got bored with the self-stimulatory behavior of repetitive spelling.

Not all self-stimulatory behaviors transition as smoothly as the spelling transitioned into speaking. Sometimes the behavior has no purpose other than addressing a sensory need. A behavior like flapping objects is an example of a stim that would be used as a motivator. The child is allowed free time following an activity during which he can play independently (he'll spend that time flapping). The therapist does not redirect the child's self-stimulatory behaviors during the playtime.

Now, you might be wondering ....

16. What sensory issues affect autistic & PDD children? **Page # 27**
18. How do self-stimulatory behaviors involve the senses? **Page # 29**
19. What is perseveration? **Page # 31**
35. How are positive and negative reinforcement used in therapy? **Page # 53**
24. What is non-verbal imitation? **Page # 37**

QUESTION 75

What strategies are used to reduce self-stimulatory behaviors?

A therapist can work in collaboration with the child's team to determine what interventions to use to reduce self-stimulatory behaviors. It is not realistic to expect the behaviors to be completely eliminated because they reinforce and stabilize the child. However, it is important to reduce self-stimulatory behaviors if they interfere with the child's ability to focus on therapy or if the child is obsessed with them.

Simple redirection is a good strategy for reducing self-stimulatory behaviors. If a therapist draws too much attention to the behavior, the child will focus on that behavior. A therapist may simply redirect a behavior by continuing the task at hand and prompting the child to pay attention.

When it involves verbal prompts, the therapist addresses the activity. For example, with a child that repeatedly flaps his hands, the therapist would briefly say, "no flapping," while continuing with an excercise.

A therapist may also use physical prompts without saying anything. If the child is scratching, the therapist may simply put his hand over the child's. This is often very effective. I like to use physical prompts in some cases, but the least intrusive method is verbal. The child may not process the verbal prompt and it may need to be repeated or accompanied by a physical prompt.

If the child has not engaged in any self-stimulatory behaviors in awhile, it is a good idea to praise or reward him. This will reinforce the absence of the behavior. A therapist could say, "Nice, quiet hands!" while giving the child a treat. This is particularly effective if the child had previously been redirected from engaging self-stimulatory behavior.

When it comes to running therapy, it is important that self-stimulatory behaviors never become such an issue that the child loses focus on the drill or activity. Many of the methods a therapist uses to control therapy and keep the client attentive are no different than actions taken by a teacher in an elementary classroom. It is still important to remember that the child with whom a therapist works has natural difficulty with communication. I have spent hours redirecting a client from a certain behavior, progressing therapy forward the entire time.

Now, you might be wondering ....

17. What are tactile, vestibular and proprioceptive systems? **Page # 28**
18. How do self-stimulatory behaviors involve the senses? **Page # 29**

What strategies are used to reduce verbal perseveration?

QUESTION 76

Perseveration, the act of making repetitive statements and asking the same questions over and over again, is a behavior that needs to be addressed systematically. First, the specific behavior must be identified. The family may identify the verbal perseveration while working with the behavior specialist or the team may notice the repetition after therapy has begun.

I have actually seen perseverated questions and statements listed in a treatment plan, with the goal set as reducing the number of times that these questions are asked or the statements are made. However, perseveration can fall under different specific goals. When the perseveration is listed under *compliance*, the focus is encouraging the child to follow verbal cues and redirect the behavior. Under *communication*, the therapist encourages the child to use appropriate statements instead and under *social goals*, the perseveration is approached much like a self-stimulatory behavior such as hand-flapping and the goal is to reduce the number of times the behavior is initiated.

Whatever goal the behavior is linked to, one of the most effective strategies for encouraging the child to reduce perseveration is through reinforcement. The therapist catches the child asking appropriate questions and making appropriate statements and rewards him immediately. I have seen programs that use timers. The therapist sets the timer for one or two minutes and gives the child a sticker if the timer goes off without his asking repeated questions or making repeated statements.

Another approach that helps the child see the ramifications of the perseverations is a traffic light coloring page. Each time the child asks the repeated question, the therapist colors part of the traffic light. The therapist begins with green, then yellow, then red. If the red section of the traffic light is colored, the child loses a play activity or other reinforcement.

I have also used marbles. I would bring twenty marbles to each of the child's sessions and put them in a bowl for her. Each time she would perseverate, she would lose one marble. This was very effective for her because she was very motivated by the marbles and the consequence was visual and immediate. She did not want those marbles to be taken out of her bowl.

Planned ignoring is another effective approach, especially if the behavior is an issue of compliance. If the perseveration is a self-stimulatory behavior it will continue if ignored. However, if the function of the behavior is to get a reaction, it will gradually reduce over time if it is ignored.

The English language is complicated. A child may perseverate on a statement because it is confusing to him. In these instances, the therapist must deal with issues of figurative and idiomatic language, helping the client to learn the meaning behind this form of communication.

Now, you might be wondering ....

16. What sensory issues affect autistic & PDD children? **Page # 27**
17. What are tactile, vestibular and proprioceptive systems? **Page # 28**
18. How do self-stimulatory behaviors involve the senses? **Page # 29**
19. What is perseveration? **Page # 31**
69. What activities help a child develop cognitive processes? **Page # 108**
70. What are some strategies for working with families? **Page # 110**
72. What are some strategies for teaching replacement behaviors? **Page # 113**
73. What strategies are used for teaching idioms? **Page # 115**
74. What strategies are used to motivate autistic children? **Page # 117**
75. What strategies are used to reduce self-stimulatory behaviors? **Page # 118**

Understanding, "Perseveration"

Perseveration is probably the most recognizable behavior exhibited by children suffering from an autism spectrum disorder. For many people who work outside of the field, perseveration is also the main behavior with which they acknowledge autism.

The behavior manifests itself as a repetitive act, such as hand flapping, saying a word or performing any other specific activity repeatedly, regardless of whether or not the initial stimuli that caused the behavior is maintained. Perseveration is of utmost importance to any professional working with autism spectrum children because this is a behavior that must be controlled and shaped. Remember, the main goal of a program such as Wraparound is to help the child to learn ways to better function in social situations. For the autistic child, perseveration is normally caused by the need to stimulate underactive physiological systems, but in a social environment, these actions can wreak havoc. This is the reason that behaviors such as these are given such a large amount of attention in the program.

What are some strategies to help an autistic child integrate sensory information?

QUESTION 77

A therapist can determine how the child takes in sensory information by the nature of their self-stimulatory behaviors. For example, if the child rocks back-and-forth and spins, the therapist can infer that the child is trying to stimulate the vestibular system. The therapist can choose to engage the child in appropriate activities that address the child's needs. If the child is trying to stimulate the vestibular system, playing on a swing or merry-go-round would address the need.

Sensory integration techniques can be valuable tools for addressing self-stimulatory problems. There are a number of sensory integration activities that can be used to address self-stimulatory behaviors:

1. Visual stimulatory behaviors
The therapist can use a hand-held windmill, engaging the child with the object by spinning it when the child communicates that he wants more. There are many mechanical toys that move objects up a ramp then release objects down a slide that can be used in therapy. Items like lava lamps and bubble machines are great visual stimulation.

Lite-Brite is a visual activity that engages the child. It also requires fine motor skills.

2. Auditory stimulatory behaviors
Music is a wonderful tool for engaging a child in appropriate auditory stimulation. The child may play instruments as well. Many children love these kinds of activities.

3. Olfactory and gustatory stimulatory behaviors
Scented bubbles, flowers and scratch-and-sniff stickers are examples of appropriate olfactory stimulation. Lollipops, popsicles and swizzle sticks are examples of appropriate gustatory stimulation.

4. Tactile stimulatory behaviors
Sand and water tables are very popular with children and they really engage the child's tactile sense. A therapist may put various materials in a container and encourage the child to feel the items. The materials should vary in texture from silk to sandpaper. Bubble wrap is a good item to use for tactile activities. If the child does not have the fine motor skills necessary to pop the bubbles, he can walk on the bubble wrap.

5. Vestibular and proprioceptive behaviors
The therapist may engage the child in activities like swinging, sliding, and climbing or the child may sit on a merry-go-round, ride a rocking horse or jump on a trampoline to address vestibular sensory needs.

The therapist can use deep pressure, including hugs and pressing pillows against the child or the therapist can use games like tug-of-war to address proprioceptive sensory needs.

Not all socially acceptable self-stimulatory behaviors are appropriate in all settings. A person should not bite his nails while preparing a meal. A person should not smoke on an airplane. We learn how to suppress our stimulatory urges at certain times. A therapist can encourage the child who engages in self-stimulatory behaviors to limit the behavior. Engaging the child in sensory integration activities like the ones listed above will help the child reduce self-stimulatory behaviors, but the child may need further prompting to encourage him to save the behaviors for specific times and places.

Self-stimulatory behaviors are extremely motivating. A teenager will do chores to earn time to play a video game. In the same sense, a therapist can use self-stimulatory behaviors and sensory integration to motivate a client.

Now, you might be wondering ....

16. What sensory issues affect autistic & PDD children? **Page # 27**
17. What are tactile, vestibular and proprioceptive systems? **Page # 28**

Jumbled sensory information

Can you imagine what it would be like to walk outside on a bright, sunny, spring day, throw your arms out wide and turn your face to the sky only to hear the terrifying, earth shaking, roar of a tidal wave engulfing you? For children that suffer with many of the autism spectrum disorders, the pathways for their senses are jumbled. A child with Asperger's could possibly walk outside on a sunny day and, 'hear,' the sunlight. An autistic child may put on a certain type of sweater and their sense of touch becomes so heightened that the clothing is virtually unbearable.

If you begin a career working with special needs children, it is absolutely necessary for you to understand that the people you are working with do not experience the world the same way that you do. Your ultimate goal is to help them to better function in their environment, even in situations where you can't entirely know what it is that they are experiencing.

Your Questions Answered on...

THERAPY: DIFFERENT SETTINGS

78. What goals do therapists address during a visit to a playground?
   Page # 124

79. How are sensory needs addressed during a trip to the playground?
   Page # 126

80. What is the therapist's role in the classroom?
   Page # 128

81. What are some general rules the therapist follows in the classroom?
   Page # 130

82. How is the treatment plan addressed in community settings?
   Page # 132

QUESTION 78

What goals do therapists address during a visit to a playground?

After I arrived home from work one evening, my husband asked me what I did that day. I said that I went to the playground and stopped for some ice cream. He said, "I thought you had to work today!" I did work that day and I accomplished a lot.

It may seem strange that a jaunt to a playground and a visit to an ice cream stand are considered work, but it is when providing therapy for a special needs child. There are a number of ways to address goals in a community setting and there are countless interventions a therapist can use while working in the community.

Here's how goals are addressed during a typical visit to a playground:

1. **Compliance** - The therapist can address compliance goals during a visit to a playground by using verbal prompts and physical prompts to help the child follow adult directions. The verbal and physical prompts help the child with safety awareness as well. Common verbal cues include:

~**Wait**. The child is given the, "wait," command while getting ready to enter the playground and while preparing to use the playground equipment. If the child does not follow through, the therapist uses physical prompts like putting her hand on his shoulders while giving the command to, "wait."

~**Stop**. *Stop* is an essential and challenging verbal cue for the child to follow during a community outing. It is best to keep the child close while working on this command because you may often have to physically halt the child.

~**All done**. Getting the client to go to the playground is not usually much of a challenge. Getting them to leave the playground is. The difficulty with prompting the child to leave the park is finding adequate reinforcement. The payoff for following, "all done," is leaving the playground, which is not appealing to any five year old. Visual aids and reinforcing rewards are helpful, hence the trip to the ice cream stand. The therapist can use a picture of ice cream to help the child transition.

2. **Communication** - The therapist continually prompts the child to use words or sign language while immersed in so many desired activities. The therapist encourages the child to communicate that he wants to continue an activity by using, "more." It is a good environment to introduce the word, "want," and others, such as, *swing, slide* and *help*.

3. **Play** - The therapist can encourage the child to initiate play by using visual and

verbal cues. For example, verbal cues like, "You'd better run," or, "I'm going to get you," can be used to get the child interested in a chasing game. It is essential that the child understands, "stop," before playing a chasing game, so use the game as a tool for teaching, "stop," first. This is done by using the verbal cues, chasing and saying, "stop," while halting the child and giving rewards. Most children find tickles rewarding in this play activity.

4. **Social skills** - The therapist prompts the child to make eye contact and respond to questions. The therapist can encourage the child to initiate and reciprocate play with other children through modeling and prompts. The client also learns to wait for others to finish an activity before engaging in it himself. For example, he has to wait for another child to get off a swing before he can swing.

Now, you might be wondering ....

1. What is a therapist (TSS)? **Page # 6**
68. After skills are mastered, how does a therapist generalize these to different settings? **Page # 107**
70. What are some strategies for working with families? **Page # 110**
79. How are sensory needs addressed during a trip to the playground? **Page # 126**
80. What is the therapist's role in the classroom? **Page # 128**
81. What are some general rules the therapist follows in the classroom? **Page # 130**
82. How is the treatment plan addressed in community settings? **Page # 132**

Early signs of autism spectrum disorders

Most children are incredibly social. They make eye contact, grab fingers, and move to interact with others. One of the first signs that a child may be autistic is the apparent lack of these behaviors. Autistic children tend to prefer being alone, they form unusual bonds with parents and other family members, shy away from touch or forgo social interaction altogether. They also tend to be very quiet and passive, with little need of attention from others.

While many children exhibit all of these behaviors (lack of social behavior, etc.), the autistic child's behaviors are remarkeably more pronounced. In all, the most prominent sign of autism is a complete lack of interest in others.

How are sensory needs addressed during a trip to the playground?

There are a number of sensory integration activities that can be used while visiting a playground. The child is immersed in sensations when he is outside. A breeze brushes against his skin. The sun is warm on his face. The rays from the sun peek through the leaves and they make a soothing rustling sound as they sway. The scent of freshly cut grass and the smell of flowers fill the air. The child has just arrived at the playground and nearly all of his senses have been stimulated.

The therapist can also use the playground to address sensory integration needs, such as:

1. Visual sensory integration activities involve information received through the eyes.

Visual sensory integration is closely related to the vestibular system. The child experiences the sensation of swinging on a swing visually as well as experiencing the motion. Any activity that involves movement like slides and merry-go-rounds also address the visual sense.

2. Auditory sensory integration activities involve information received through the ears.

The therapist can encourage the child to drum on the slide after he reaches the bottom. The therapist can make a sound as the child slides or swings. Everything from the sound of other children on the playground to the sound of the actual child playing addresses the auditory sense.

3. Tactile sensory integration activities involve information received through touch.

The therapist can play a chasing game and tickle the child when she reaches him. The therapist can encourage the child to experience different textures through touching a tree, grass or a rubber tire. Any activity that involves texture and touch involves the tactile sense.

4. Gustatory sensory integration activities involve information received through taste.

This sense is difficult to address in a playground setting other than encouraging the child to use a water fountain. However, the sense of taste and the sense of smell are closely linked.

5. Olfactory sensory integration activities are tied to gustatory behaviors.

The therapist doesn't really need to do anything to engage the child's olfactory sense. Fragrances are inherent to any outdoor activity. The therapist can bring the smell of freshly cut grass or the smell of flowers to the child's attention through verbal prompts and exaggerating a sniffing motion.

Sensory integration activities help a child calm and organize his behavior. The child uses the activities as a release. Once sensory needs are met, the child can focus on following through with directions and the child can focus on his environment. Sensory integration is a good approach to facilitate attention and compliance goals.

Now, you might be wondering ....

1. What is a therapist (TSS)? **Page # 6**
49. What is the treatment plan? **Page # 76**
68. After skills are mastered, how does a therapist generalize these to different settings? **Page # 107**
70. What are some strategies for working with families? **Page # 110**

Education 101

Even though much of what you find in this guide applies to psychology, making it appear that a career spent working with special needs children is best served through a strong foundation in that field of study, don't count out those classes in education.

Many of the skills you would use working with autistic children are employed everyday by teachers in the classroom, though often on a less overt scale. Dealing with issues such as a child's inability to understand concepts, their anxiety and stress or simply explaining complex social situations in simple, easy to understand, terms are all skills that educators work to develop. These same issues are crucial to working with special needs children. Taking an interest in the science behind education can help you to have a greater effect in your efforts.

QUESTION 80: What is the therapist's role in the classroom?

A therapist's role in the classroom is a little different than his role in the home and community settings. The therapist is a mental healthcare provider, not an academic instructor. The therapist works in collaboration with the teacher and uses the behavior specialist as a mediator.

The child's behavior specialist, family and relevant school staff members attend interagency meetings, where a number of issues are discussed:

Goals and objectives

The group discusses the goals and objectives in the child's treatment plan in the school setting. The behavior specialist outlines the specific goals that the treatment plan addresses in the school setting. The goals usually address *compliance, attention, communication* and *social needs*.

The role of the therapist in the classroom

The therapist's role will be discussed (and determined) in interagency meetings. The behavior specialist explores different strategies and techniques that the therapist will use in the classroom setting, focusing on behavioral issues, not academic. Usually, the therapist deals with any behavior that disrupts the classroom environment and interferes with the client's or with other students' learning. Examples of goals that are addressed in the child's school setting include:

1. Compliance - Under compliance goals the therapist may address transitions. The child may have difficulty ending one task and moving on to another. He may have difficulty coming back into the classroom after recess. He may refuse to wait in line or he may simply refuse to follow directions.

2. Attention - Under attention goals the therapist may address completion of tasks. The child may have difficulty paying attention to a speaker. He may be unable to focus on a worksheet or classroom activity.

3. Communication - The child may have difficulty processing spoken directions. He may require visual aids to help him understand what is expected. He may need encouragement to use words to access wants and needs.

4. Social - The child may have difficulty initiating and reciprocating play. He may need prompting to help him play appropriately with others, take turns and wait. He may have difficulty making eye contact or using appropriate voice tone.

Criteria for fading

After the therapist's role in the classroom is addressed, the criteria for fading services in the school setting are addressed. The therapist may work with a child for a semester or for a couple years, depending on the child's needs and progress.

Data collection and paperwork

During the interagency meeting, the behavior specialist, family and school personnel establish a procedure for data and paperwork completion. The group determines where forms will be located and how signatures will be collected.

The beauty of the process is that the forms, procedures and information are there for the therapist. Just as the program book outlines the specific goals, drills, activities and interventions in the home setting, everything for the school setting is organized and ready to go. All the therapist has to do is use interventions when appropriate.

Now, you might be wondering ....

1. What is a therapist (TSS)? **Page # 6**
68. After skills are mastered, how does a therapist generalize these to different settings? **Page # 107**
70. What are some strategies for working with families? **Page # 110**
81. What are some general rules the therapist follows in the classroom? **Page # 130**
82. How is the treatment plan addressed in community settings? **Page # 132**

Why the rise in autism cases?

The number of people diagnosed with autism has risen significantly over the last decade, leading many to wonder if this occurance is the result of environmental factors or simply a change in the way that acceptable diagnostic symptoms have been expanded upon. This debate can have some serious ramifications. If the occurance of autism is actually increasing because of environmental factors, it means that an increase in the research surrounding the possible causes and early interventions would be more fruitful than working to expand available treatment options. Throughout your career you will find that the interests of different organizations are intertwined with the way that this debate progresses.

QUESTION 81

What are some general rules the therapist follows in the classroom?

The most important thing to understand about providing treatment for special needs children in the school is realizing that eventually the therapist will not be in the classroom at all. Their involvement is temporary, so the teacher should decide how they want classroom therapy to be arranged. Work in a classroom can go terribly wrong if the therapist does not work in collaboration with the teacher.

Therapist's role is specific.

The therapist has specific functions in the school setting. The role depends on the child's treatment plan, but some general rules apply when providing therapy in a classroom. On the whole, the therapist serves as a support system for the child in school, working in collaboration with the child's teachers in order to support the child and meet his needs. The rest of the team coordinates with the school officials to reach a clear, mutual, understanding of how treatment is to be delivered in the school setting.

Remember HIPAA.

The therapist should never infringe on the client's right to privacy. It is good practice to keep all conversations related to the child's treatment plan when in the school. A simple statement such as, "he's much worse at home," is noncompliant to HIPAA standards.

Keep journals objective and measurable.

The behavior specialist usually includes a communication log between the child's treatment team. It is best to keep information in the journal objective. I often write things like, "The child was really frustrated during math," but I also write why I think that he was frustrated. Adding something simple such as, "as evidenced by breaking his pencil," gives support to the statement. Writing statements like, "the child raised her hand three times and the teacher never called on her," accomplishes nothing but disharmony with the team. The statement suggests that the child is being ignored, while that may not be the case. In all, try to keep the teacher in mind when recording data and remember that they have an entire classroom of students to consider.

Dress and act professionally.

Every day is casual day in the home setting. The therapist may get involved with physical activities in the home setting and the therapist needs to dress comfortably and appropriately. In the school setting, the therapist needs to follow the school's dress codes for their staff. This may include no open-toed shoes or no jeans.

Check in with the office.

Even if you have been visiting the school for months, it is good practice to consistently check in with the office. Sometimes the office personnel have important information for the therapist, including the child's possible absence. If the therapist goes into the classroom and the child is not there, he has just disrupted the class. You may not feel like a visitor in the school after working there for awhile, but you are.

The therapist follows the teacher's lead.

It is a good idea to keep communication open with the teacher. It is important to establish a classroom procedure that is consistent with all therapists on the case. If one therapist is sitting in the back of the classroom and the other is sitting right next to the child, there is a rift in communication between the staff members. Touching base with the teacher's preferences right from the beginning will help establish a system.

Some teachers like to incorporate the therapist into their class. These teachers usually introduce the therapist to the class as a helper. I worked with a teacher who put my client's visual schedule in front of the class and used it as a schedule for the entire class to use. The schedule flowed seamlessly with the teacher's organized approach. It helped the client transition and it helped the client understand what to expect while functioning in the same capacity for the rest of the classroom.

Other teachers like for the therapist to stay out of sight. Many of these teachers appreciate it if you develop signals for them to use to give you cues as to when they would like you to intervene. This is a little more challenging for the therapist, but once the system is in order, things run smoothly.

Now, you might be wondering ....

1. What is a therapist (TSS)? **Page # 6**
68. After skills are mastered, how does a therapist generalize these to different settings? **Page # 107**
70. What are some strategies for working with families? **Page # 110**
78. What goals do therapists address during a visit to a playground? **Page # 124**
80. What is the therapist's role in the classroom? **Page # 128**
82. How is the treatment plan addressed in community settings? **Page # 132**

QUESTION 82

How is the treatment plan addressed in community settings?

Every plan for treatment is child-specific. In many cases the treatment plan includes community outings as part of the child's therapy. Community sessions may appear quite different from a session in the home, but the same goals usually apply. The behavior specialist includes interventions to use in a community setting. The therapist does not usually use a program book in the community, but she collects data about the child's behavior and takes notes on the child's progress.

Let's look at how a therapist works to shape behavior in a community setting. In this example, the treatment team is working with a child who is diagnosed with **pervasive developmental disorder-not otherwise specified**. The girl is high-functioning, but has difficulty developing relationships with peers and she has difficulty with communication. She also has a tendency to repeat the same questions over and over again at inappropriate times in attempts to initiate conversation. The treatment plan outlines *play skills, compliance* and *social communication* as goals in the community setting. This means that the therapist and the team are trying to work with the child to get him to play with other children, to comply with instructions and interact with others (initiate conversation, not repeat words, etc.).

In this instance, let's say the child attends a church camp every week. The child would be accompanied by a therapist and this would be thought of as a community based shift. In these situations, the therapist will try to use interventions that are as non-intrusive as possible.

During part of community shift, the children are engaging in a series of games, like water balloons and dodge ball. The therapist would not thrust the child into the activities right away, so the first week they may just try to get the client cheering for other children. Rewards would be given to the child for cheering. After the child cheers without prompts, the therapist models standing in line with the other children, gradually prompting and rewarding the child. The goal is for the child to eventually participate in play activities with peers.

It may take months for the child to participate with the other children. In this example, the child's behavior has been shaped to meet the compliance and play skills goals. The therapist can also prompt the child to greet others and reciprocate conversation, meeting the social communication goals.

Now, you might be wondering ....

1. What is a therapist (TSS)? **Page # 6**
9. What treatment program is used most frequently? **Page # 16**
39. How do drills adhere to the treatment plan? **Page # 60**
68. After skills are mastered, how does a therapist generalize these to different settings? **Page # 107**
70. What are some strategies for working with families? **Page # 110**
78. What goals do therapists address during a visit to a playground? **Page # 124**
79. How are sensory needs addressed during a trip to the playground? **Page # 126**
80. What is the therapist's role in the classroom? **Page # 128**
81. What are some general rules the therapist follows in the classroom? **Page # 130**

Is autism inherited?

With the debate raging regarding the dominant causes for autism, asking whether or not it is inherited may seem a little hasty. Generally, all afflictions and, for that matter, traits, are to a degree inherited. Researchers accept that how we develop is determined by a combination of genes and environment. At most, a certain genetic structure predisposes us to certain behaviors or diseases, but personal actions and environment play a large part in whether traits manifest.

Currently, researchers accept that there are five chromosomal regions, chromosome 2, 3, 7 and 15 as well as the X chromosome, that are prevalent among autistics, making it very difficult to argue against the inheritability of the disorder. For someone working with special needs children, the important thing to understand is that you may find family members exhibiting some of the behaviors associated with autism. Recent studies have shown a tendency for families to develop autism-spectrum behaviors. In these cases, the difficulty is not just in working with the child, but also being prepared to work with the family.

PAPERWORK & TRAINING

Your Questions Answered on...

83. Do therapists fill out a lot of paperwork? **Page # 135**

84. What are supervision meetings and why are they important? **Page # 136**

85. How many training hours are required every year? **Page # 137**

86. How are shifts organized in increments of time? **Page # 139**

87. What is HIPPA? **Page # 140**

Do therapists fill out a lot of paperwork?

QUESTION 83

Between shift reports, encounter forms, ABC charts, forms to record hours worked and everything else, a therapist can spend a significant amount of time filling out paperwork.

Different therapists approach this aspect of the job differently. With regards to paperwork relative to the therapy (such as an ABC chart or bubble sheets), these need filled out during therapy. The purpose of these forms is to record necessary data that affects therapy. Both the behaviorist and the case manager will use the recorded data to make decisions about the progress of the therapy.

Compared to other types of careers, a therapist spends relatively little time filling out paperwork that isn't related directly to the task at hand (such as the bubble sheets related to discrete trial drills).

As far as the other paperwork, it may seem as if there is a lot of it, but the forms are direct, clean and objective. It takes a few seconds to fill in information as you go. The best way to handle it is a little at a time, rather than saving up the forms to fill in all at once.

One very important thing to remember is that a large part of the therapist's job takes part on-site. With the exception of meetings and mandatory training, you spend very little time in the office (at least compared to many other professions). The last thing you want is to have to go into the office to fix some time sheets that weren't filled in properly. Therapist should try to always fill in paperwork properly because this information is used by other professionals as they try to meet their goals.

Now, you might be wondering ....

1. What is a therapist (TSS)? **Page # 6**
2. What qualifications does a therapist need? **Page # 8**
51. How do bubble sheets fit into the therapist's work? **Page # 80**
52. What does a target list look like? **Page # 82**

QUESTION 84

What are supervision meetings & why are they important?

Therapists work one-on-one with the children, most often without supervision. Each week, the therapist attends a supervision meeting. Supervision meetings help the therapist stay informed about the organization she works for, while also helping the professional to stay updated on current practices in the treatment of autism spectrum disorders.

The first supervision meeting addresses mandatory topics for the month. Mandatory topics usually revolve around paperwork, office information and standard procedures for working with clients.

Supervision meetings also include staff discussions about cases. During case review supervision meetings, each therapist takes a turn discussing his clients. The discussions involve the child's progress, strategies that work well with the child and stumbling blocks in the child's therapy. The group attending the meeting brainstorms ideas for improving the child's program and sessions.

Occasionally, the behavior specialist conducts on-site supervision. During an on-site supervision, the therapist works with the child as usual. This is often more difficult than it seems. I have found that an observer in the room changes the dynamics in the session but it is important to try to make the shift run as usual. These sessions give the behavior specialist an opportunity to make suggestions and develop new strategies. There may be a simple solution to why the child is struggling with a certain drill or activity.

Sometimes a different perspective is very valuable. I worked with a child who would have a tantrum towards the end of some drills. The behavior specialist told me that I tended to say, "one more," towards the end of each drill. If the child gave an incorrect response, we had to repeat the trial, so there would often be another trial following the, "one more." This repetition led to negative behaviors. An on-site supervision solved this ongoing problem.

Now, you might be wondering ....

1. What is a therapist (TSS)? **Page # 6**
3. What is a case manager? **Page # 9**
5. What is a behavioral specialist? **Page # 11**
7. What types of conflicts arise within a treatment team? **Page # 13**
8. What are the benefits in working with special needs children? **Page # 15**
9. What treatment program is used most frequently? **Page # 16**

How many training hours are required every year?

The agency or organization may have specific trainings that have to be repeated each year, along with a mandatory number of continuing education hours. Twenty hours a year is common, with many of these available on-line or in seminar format. In terms of a career, this is a relatively low number of mandatory training hours. Not filling required training hours may lead to suspension, so it is important to keep current on training hours.

Refresher trainings often concern topics that require the staff to have the most up-to-date information in order to continue working. Refresher trainings can include **First Aid and CPR**. First Aid certification usually is refreshed every two years. CPR training is refreshed each year. Some organizations do not make First Aid and CPR training mandatory, but the organizations will most likely accept the training as credit towards your twenty hours for the year.

OSHA is common mandatory training. OSHA is the Occupational Safety and Health Administration. It involves safety procedures while working in the field. OSHA is relevant to therapist because it is crucial to utilize the safest approach to working with families. A therapist should have the information necessary to quickly deal with health related issues that range from blood borne pathogens and hazardous materials to the common cold.

Safe Crisis Management is another training that is often mandated by an organization that employs therapists. Refreshing Safe Crisis Management techniques keeps the staff members up-to-date on the latest procedures for dealing with a crisis. It also guarantees that all staff members follow the same procedures and adhere to the child's treatment plan.

Corporate compliance may be included with a therapist's yearly training. Corporate compliance has to be renewed every year because the staff needs to keep current with the standard policies the agency or organization follows. Corporate compliance trainings usually involve issues like the client's right to privacy, accuracy of paperwork and accurate reporting of the hours that a therapist works.

The mandatory trainings can take up to three hours each, so the employees may only need to find eleven hours of training on their own. However, most organizations offer training throughout the year. Usually employees are compensated for hours spent in training and topics can range from pervasive developmental disorders to partnering with families.

Information about the autism rights movement

If you decide to pursue a career working with special needs children, you'll most likely spend your time working with other professionals that support the use of ABA based programs. It is important to know, however, that an entire culture surrounds the occurance of autism with people taking various sides and holding very different opinions as to the best course of action.

The term, 'aspies,' refers to high-functioning autistics or individuals with Asperger's. Groups such as *Aspies for Freedom* work against the drive for an autism cure, making the argument that autism is not so much a disorder as a different way of perciewing and experiencing the world.

Th main conflict is between organizations such as *Aspies for Freedom* and others such as *Cure Autism Now*. An important thing to remember with regards to this debate is that most groups advocating the acceptance of autistics rather than treatment are incredibly high functioning. Individuals that work with autistics are normally helping children that have severe problems and would not be able to function in the world without help.

How are shifts organized in increments of time?

QUESTION 86

The behavior specialist determines the activities, but it is generally up to the therapist to organize everything that needs done into a complete shift. For example, a child may have a lot of sensory issues and the behavior specialist includes sensory integration activities that need to be done three times each hour. When the therapist puts together the child's schedule, he should include a sensory integration activity every fifteen minutes or so. The child may have equipment in the therapy room like a trampoline or a swing. During the sensory integration activities, the therapist encourages the child to make eye contact and prompts the child to communicate whether he wants to continue or whether he wants the activity to stop.

The child's schedule may look like this:

SWING   LETTERS   PUZZLE   TRAMPOLINE   NUMBERS   BREAK

Again, the number of activities included in the schedule depends on the child. The *Letters* drill will probably only take a few minutes. There are usually ten trials in a drill, but if the child repeatedly gives correct responses, a therapist may only use four or five trials. The child is directed to *go play* for a couple minutes as reinforcement. A puzzle can take anywhere from five to ten minutes depending on the child. A therapist can have the child complete more than one puzzle if the child finishes quickly. Between swinging and trampoline is about thirty minutes worth of therapy. Time goes very quickly during a shift that is broken down into fifteen minute increments. The above schedule represents about forty five minutes.

As you may have noticed, many things happen very quickly in therapy. Over the course of three hours, dozens of activities are covered, each relating to various treatment goals. Surprisingly, creating a schedule that flows into increments of time will become second nature as you become familiar with the child. When I create a schedule for a newer client, I cushion it with an extra activity. The child will tolerate an activity being taken off the schedule much easier than he will an activity being added to the schedule. When I'm not sure how long things will take, I add a couple activities from the child's maintenance program onto the schedule.

Now, you might be wondering ....

1. What is a therapist (TSS)? **Page # 6**
3. What is a case manager? **Page # 9**
5. What is a behavioral specialist? **Page # 11**

QUESTION 87

What is HIPPA?

HIPPA - HIPPA is an act first introduced in 1996 as the Health Insurance Portability and Accountability Act. The Health Insurance Portability and Accountability Act officially took effect in 2003 and involves the client's right to privacy and the healthcare provider's responsibility to protect the client's privacy. Since Wraparound and other autism treatment programs are mental health services, employees who work with the program must adhere to HIPPA standards. Basically, a therapist is not allowed to disclose any identifiable information about her clients. For example, my husband knows what I do for a living. Since he knows that I am a therapist, I can not say hello to my clients if I see them out in public. I have to wait until the child or the child's parents approach me. They can introduce me as a friend or as a therapist. It is completely up to them. They may not approach at all. I would be noncompliant to HIPPA standards if I said, "That's the little girl I work with on the weekends. Isn't she cute?" The child's therapy is protected by the Health Insurance Portability and Accountability Act.

Adhering to HIPAA standards is not always easy. You may find yourself in a public setting surrounded by people during a shift and need to complete the shift report and get signatures. The law makes it necessary to find a private spot to complete paperwork.

You may also find yourself dodging questions about your client. In some cases, you will be in a community or school setting and the parents will not be around. The teacher or group leader is supposed to sign the encounter form because that person is present when the therapist leaves. The child's teacher is part of his treatment team and is probably privy to much of the child's information, but it is still necessary to not divulge any information that is not relevant to the school setting. For example, saying, "The child behaves much worse at home!" is noncompliant to HIPPA standards.

I was once injured during a shift and I had to go to the emergency room. When the hospital staff asked where I was, I felt silly, but I couldn't disclose the location of the incident. Once I mentioned HIPPA, no further questions were asked. All of the information about the minor injury was included in an incident report.

Now, you might be wondering ....

85. How many training hours are required every year? **Page # 137**
100. I think I want to work with special needs children, where should I start? **Page # 159**

Your Questions Answered on...

REFERENCE

88. What organizations support careers involved in working with special needs children? **Page # 142**

89. What books are available to help me learn more about working with special needs children? **Page # 143**

90. What are some important moments in the history of autism treatment? **Page # 144**

91. Where can I find employment opportunities? **Page # 146**

92. Where can I find current information related to autism studies? **Page # 147**

93. What are some important moments in applied behavioral analysis? **Page # 148**

94. What are some methods for autism treatment aside from ABA? **Page # 150**

95. Where are some websites where I can learn more about Wraparound? **Page # 152**

96. What are some different roles that I can take in a career spent working with special needs children? **Page # 153**

97. What education is required for the different roles you can take working with special needs children? **Page # 155**

98. What are some related fields that I can pursue after getting experience working with special needs children? **Page # 156**

99. What are some notable organizations related to the history of working with special needs children? **Page # 158**

100. I think I want to work with special needs children, where should I start? **Page # 159**

101. What's next? **Page # 160**

QUESTION 88

What organizations support careers involved in working with special needs children?

There are numerous resources available to learn more about careers involved in working with special needs children. Below are just a few that can help provide you with more information about working in any number of roles within this field:

1. **The Council for Exceptional Children (CEC)**: Hailed as the single largest professional organization dedicated to helping persons with exceptionalities, CEC advocates on behalf of special education programs, while representing a number of types of professionals working in the field of special education. 1110 North Glebe Road, Suite 300, Arlington, VA 22201, Voice phone: 703-620-3660, service@cec.sped.org,

www.cec.sped.org

2. **Association for Behavior Analysis International** : ABA International is a member based professional organization that supports the growth of Behavior Analysis. 1219 South Park Street, Kalamazoo, MI 49001, Phone: (269) 492-9310, E-mail: mail@abainternational.org

www.abainternational.org

3. **Autism Society of America (ASA):** ASA is one of the oldest autism related groups in the United States. With dozens of chapters nationwide, this is an excellent organization for autism professions.

www.autism-society.org

The following are some regional websites and directories related to autism and special needs children:

1. www.icdl.com/resources
2. www.theautismprogram.org
3. www.autismtoday.com

Now, you might be wondering ....

94. What are some methods for autism treatment aside from ABA? **Page #150**
100. I think I want to work with special needs children, where should I start? **Page #159**
101. What's next? **Page #160**

What books are available to help me learn more about working with special needs children?

QUESTION 89

There are literally hundreds of different books available to help you learn more about ABA, special needs related conditions and different career fields associated with these issues. The following books are must-haves that will provide you with an excellent foundation in the approach taken by therapists, behaviorists and case managers in dealing with special needs disorders, especially autism and PDD:

1. **A Work in Progress: Behavior Management Strategies & A Curriculum for Intensive Behavioral Treatment of Autism (Paperback) by Ron Leaf, John McEachin, Jaisom D. Harsh, ISBN: 0966526600**

"A Work in Progress," is an incredible guide for parents or professionals in need of ABA reference teaching materials. The book covers everything from how interventions work to a complete pre-developed curriculum.

2. **Teaching Individuals With Developmental Delays: Basic Intervention Techniques (Paperback) by O. Ivar Lovaas, ISBN: 0890798893**

This is a good resource to get you introduced to all of the terms and strategies for treating disorders within the autism spectrum. The book also includes information on maneuvering an autistic child through the public education system. Dr. Lovass is accredited with developing the foundation for Applied Behavioral Analysis, so this is considered to be something of a bible for the professional field as it relates to Wraparound programs.

3. **Behavioral Intervention for Young Children with Autism by Catherine Maurice, Gina Greene and Stephen C. Luce, ISBN: 0890796831**

4. **Right from the Start: Behavioral Intervention for Young Children With Autism : A Guide for Parents and Professionals by Sandra L. Harris, Mary Jane, Ph.D. Gill-Weiss, ISBN: 189062702X**

Now, you might be wondering ....

92. Where can I find current information related to autism studies? **Page # 147**

93. What are some important moments in applied behavioral analysis? **Page # 148**

QUESTION 90

What are some important moments in the history of autism?

The last half of the twenty-first century saw an incredible surge in autism research and the development of treatment methods. With so many advances in the field of Child Psychology, it's often hard for people to understand that the philosophy and experimentation related to special needs children is still in its infancy. The following timeline includes some of the most important moments in the treatment of autism and Pervasive Developmental Disorders:

1943: Leo Kanner, a child psychiatrist at Johns Hopkins Hospital in Baltimore, coined the term, "autism," from the Greek word autos, meaning self. He used this term to describe 11 children under his treatment. Kanner would go on to become one of the founders of Child Psychology in the United States.

1944: Hans Asperger, a pediatrician from Vienna, uses the word, "autism," to describe children who shared similar but milder forms of the cases reported by Kanner.

1949: Kanner publishes a paper where he attributes autism to a lack of sufficient maternal care. The idea gave autism a social component and led to a great deal of emotional stress for families with autistic children.

1950s: Bruno Bettelheim, an Austrian psychologist who taught at the University of Chicago, supported Kanner's philosophy. He wrote, *The Empty Fortress: Infantile Autism and the Birth of Self*.

1964: Bernard Rimland, also a psychologist at the University of Chicago, publicly rebuts Bettleheim's ideas in his book, *Infantile Autism: The Syndrome and Its Implications for a Neural Theory of Behavior*.

1965: The Autism Society of America is founded by Rimland. The establishment of ASA is a major step in creating a surge in Autism research and treatment for disorders.

1965: Dr. Ivar Lovaas began studying methods for treating children with autism at the UCLA Clinic for the Behavioral Treatment of Children. The Lovaas Therapy uses an ABA method called Discrete Trial Training (DTT), in which the autistic child is challenged with individual learning opportunities. After mastering a specific training trial, the child then builds upon the learned skill to tackle a more complex one. Lovaas Therapy consists of a series of distinct repeated lessons or trials taught one-to-one.

Typically the lessons are highly intensive, usually taking 30-40 hours per week, and conducted by a trained therapist in the family's home (in some cases, a much less intensive, informal approach of Lovaas Therapy may be implemented to teach specific skills such as sitting and attending).

Treatment begins with two primary goals: teaching *learning readiness* skills such as sitting in a chair and attending, and decreasing behaviors that interfere with learning, such as noncompliance, tantrums and aggression. Each trial consists of a request for the individual to perform an action, behavior, or response, and involves a consequence or reaction from the therapist. Positive reinforcers are selected by evaluating the individual's preferences - many children initially respond to rewards such as food items, however these concrete reinforcers usually are replaced as soon as possible with rewards such as praise, tickles, and hugs.

1980: The American Psychiatric Association adds autism to its Diagnostic and Statistical Manual (DSM) of Mental Disorders.

1991: Lorna Wing, a psychologist from the United Kingdom, introduced the idea that autism includes a variety of disorders. In essence, her work moved forward the idea of autism as a spectrum of disorders with varying degrees of affectation.

1992: Autism Network International is started by the combined effort of Americans Jim Sinclair and Kathy Grant and Australia's Donna Williams. ANI describes itself as, "an autistic-run self-help and advocacy organization for autistic people."

1993: Dr. Ivar Lovaas releases findings from studies conducted at UCLA Clinic for the Behavioral Treatment of Children.

1994: Asperger's syndrome is added to the DSM.

Now, you might be wondering ....

1. What is a therapist (TSS)? **Page # 6**
88. What organizations support careers involved in working with special needs children? **Page # 142**
89. What books are available to help me learn more about working with special needs children? **Page # 143**
90. What are some important moments in the history of autism treatment? **Page # 144**
91. Where can I find employment opportunities? **Page # 146**
92. Where can I find current information related to autism studies? **Page # 147**
93. What are some important moments in applied behavioral analysis? **Page # 148**

QUESTION 91

Where can I find employment opportunities?

You can find positions listed for therapeutic staff support workers, mobile therapists, behaviorists and case managers in all of the main job databases, including monster.com, careerbuilder.com and job.com. The following are some resources that are specific to working with special needs children:

1. Mentalhealth.net
2. Socialservice.com
3. Aftercollege.com

Aside from social services organizations, it is very common for professionals to find opportunities at special shcools and teaching organizations. The following web addresses are good places to find more information on the types of positions you can find at a special school, along with current employment opportunities:

1. http://trainland.tripod.com/residential.htm
2. www.thehelpgroup.org
3. www.clearhorizonsacademy.org
4. www.heartspring.org
5. www.andersonschool.org
6. www.iser.com

If you decide to work as a therapist (TSS), a good place to look for temporary employment is through a local healthcare staffing agency. These can be invaluable resources if you are relocating or just finished school and need to find opportunities. Staffing agencies do not frequently hold opportunities for positions as behavior specialists or case managers. Since these normally require a master's degree, your best bet is going to be placement through your school.

Now, you might be wondering ....

1. What is a therapist (TSS)? **Page # 6**
2. What qualifications does a therapist need? **Page # 8**
3. What is a case manager? **Page # 9**
4. What qualifications does a case manager need? **Page # 10**
5. What is a behavioral specialist? **Page # 11**
6. What qualifications does a behavioral specialist need? **Page # 12**
7. What types of conflicts arise within a treatment team? **Page # 13**
8. What are the benefits in working with special needs children? **Page # 15**

Where can I find information on recent autism studies?

QUESTION 92

Autism Research Centre - The Autism Research Centre (www.autismresearchcentre.com), is located at the School of Clinical Medicine in the Department of Psychiatry, Section of Developmental Psychiatry, at the University of Cambridge.

The ARC breaks their research initiatives into three areas:

a. Cognitive Neuroscience and Genetics
b. Epidemiology and Diagnosis
c. Intervention

Currently, the Autism Research Centre is involved in a number of research projects. This is a good place to get acquainted with the most recent findings in the world of autism and Asperger's. Most of the publications you will find through this resource require some technical knowledge, but the, "Intervention," section is a must read for anyone interested in working with special needs children. Normally, if it is a new type of therapy in the world of autism, you can find a related topic being researched in the ARC.

Some other places to find interesting research initiatives include:

CureAutismNow - Cure Autism Now (www.cureautismnow.org) is a coalition of organizations that either conduct or advocate for autism research.

Kennedy Krieger Institute - The Kennedy Krieger Institute conducts research and has educational and treatment facilities (www.kennedykrieger.org).

Now, you might be wondering ....

12. What are autism & PDD? **Page # 21**
13. What are the Pervasive Development Disorders? **Page # 22**
14. What are the similarities and differences between Asperger's syndrome and autism? **Page #24**
15. How do autistic children suffer from body awareness deficiencies? **Page # 26**
25. What deficiencies do autistic children have with auditory processing? **Page # 38**
26. What are executive function deficits? **Page # 39**

Who are some important individuals related to ABA and the treatment of autism?

Applied Behavioral Analysis, or ABA, is based on the principals of Behaviorism. ABA procedures are systematically applied to improve socially significant behavior. The system dictates that recorded data should demonstrate that the procedures were responsible for the behavioral changes.

A common misconception is that ABA is used only for the treatment of autism. In reality, different ABA concepts are wholly ingrained within our culture. Practices such as grading in classrooms (teachers awarding A's and putting stars on test papers) and companies giving bonuses are both instances of positive rewards to affect behavior - commonly used principals in the practice of Applied Behavioral Analysis.

As it applies to the use of ABA with autism and Pervasive Developmental Disorders, there are a few key moments in the history of Behaviorism that have led to the system of treatment in place today. This short history is by no means exhaustive. The following instances in the history of Behaviorism and Applied Behavioral Analysis strongly correlate to some of the most crucial aspects of ABA as it is put to practical use when working with special needs children.

1903 - Ivan Pavlov

At the 14th International Medical Congress in Madrid, Pavlov read a paper titled, "The Experimental Psychology and Psychopathology of Animals." Pavlov's groundbreaking paper described conditioned reflexes as a basic component of animal behavior. This paper led to the possibility of the objective study of psychic activity.

1913 - John Watson

One of the most important aspects of ABA is that it is DATA-DRIVEN. Applied Behavioral Anaylsis relies on maintaining strict, objective, records of behaviors and the use of these to guide future treatment. In 1913, John Watson published an article that virtually founded the branch of Psychology known as Behaviorism. Behaviorism represents a profound break from Freudian Psychology, taking a more empirical approach.

1948 - B.F. Skinner

In 1948, B.F. Skinner took a chair at Harvard where he was to conduct some of his most interesting work in the field of Psychology. As it relates to the treatment of autism, Skinner is responsible for theories related to operant conditioning. Operant conditioning describes the ways in which behaviors reinforced through stimuli are more likely to recur - a main component in the methods used by therapists to help autistic children develop behaviors that enable them to better navigate their environment.

1961 - Ole Ivar Lovaas

In 1961, Ole Ivar Lovaas accepted an assistant professor position at UCLA. Over the next two decades his work with autistic children would serve as the basis for autism treatment today. He was able to show a profound affect on numerous patients through the use of a structured treatment that used positive and negative reinforcement to shape behaviors.

Things such as slapping and screaming at patients were used as negative stimuli in the early years (these were called *aversive actions*). Such methods were later replaced with less aggressive and more effective methods.

Now, you might be wondering ....

1. What is a therapist (TSS)? **Page # 6**

Other communication disorders

Autism is just one form of communication disorder. Not surprisingly, there are a number of other disorders that are similar or at least fall within the same class. For example, aphasia is the loss of the ability to use or comprehend language. Expressive language disorder occurs with individuals that do not have a delay in non-verbal intelligence, but speaking and understanding of verbal communication is affected. Even conditions such as dyslexia, deafness and stuttering are considering to be disorders related to communication.

Throughout your career you could find yourself working with any number of disorders, depending on the type of position you decide to take, how far you pursue your education and numerous other factors. Just remember - there are many different afflictions being treated by therapists, psychologists and other professionals everyday.

QUESTION 94

What are some methods for autism treatment aside from ABA?

Throughout this book, most of the sections address autism treatment in terms of Applied Behavioral Analysis, which is also known as the Dr. Lovaas method. Though ABA is by far the most widely accepted and used method for treatment, there are a number of other methods being put into practice. Below are just a few of the more popular alternatives available for autism treatment:

1. **Pivotal Response Therapy** - PRT is ABA based, but considered to be a more naturalistic approach to autism treatment. In PRT, 'Pivotal Behaviors,' or those main behaviors on which a number of other behaviors are based, are the focus of the treatment. Because these behaviors influence a diverse area of functions, positive changes can have a ripple effect on other behaviors. PRT therapy tends to be more focused on the child, relaxed and based on the patient's personal motivations. PRT is offered through clinics and school programs.

2. **TEACCH** - Treatment and Education of Autistic and Related Communication Handicapped Children was developed in 1964 at the University of North Carolina at Chapel Hill. TEACCH is a classroom based program that relies heavily on visual skills and the tendency for autistic children to respond stongly to visual cues. Instead of using rewards for behavior modification, TEACCH emphasizes picture systems to develop organizational skills and help children better understand what is expected of them. Many researchers believe that TEACCH is an excellent program for very severe cases of autism.

3. **DIR Floortime** - DIR floortime is a home-based treatment that employs therapists to help parents and family members conduct excercises with the autistic client. The program was developed by Dr. Stanley Greenspan and Dr. Serena Wieder. DIR stands for Developmental, Individual-Difference, Relationship-Based Floortime and the goals are focused on helping children build fundamental skills needed for communication and relationships. The word, 'floortime,' is included because the parents, in this program, actually get down on the floor with the child. The excercises follow the child's interests and natural motivations.

Some critics claim there is not enough scientific research supporting the effectiveness of DIR Floortime and that children with more severe autism may not be well-served by such a child-centered program. The Floortime Foundation claims that in a review of 200 children diagnosed with autistic spectrum disorders who were treated intensively with DIR Floortime for up to six years, more than 50 percent have "become warm, engaged and loving."

DIR Floortime's founder Dr. Greenspan, has made the claim that this program was developed in response to the tendency for ABA centered program to produce robotic responses from clients. While a child who has gone through an ABA program can function much better in social situations, their responses are still trained and there is a general lack of understanding behind the purpose of the learned behaviors. DIR Floortime, through close interaction, is a more organic approach to teaching autistic children proper social behavior.

How treatment methods relate to your career - If you decide to pursue a career working with special needs children (or already have begun your career), the type of treatment program that you choose to work within is an important decision. Different methods are not only better suited to different client's, they're also better suited to different therapists and counselors. Some people have difficulty administering ABA related treatment because it is strictly regimented. Others find programs such as DIR Floortime, with its child-centered approach, too lacking in direction. If you decide on this field, make certain that the treatment program works well with your skills and ideas regarding the best way to help the client.

Now, you might be wondering ....

1. What is a therapist (TSS)? **Page # 6**
88. What organizations support careers involved in working with special needs children? **Page # 142**
89. What books are available to help me learn more about working with special needs children? **Page # 143**
90. What are some important moments in the history of autism treatment? **Page # 144**
91. Where can I find employment opportunities? **Page # 146**
92. Where can I find current information related to autism studies? **Page # 147**
93. What are some important moments in applied behavioral analysis? **Page # 148**

QUESTION 95

Where are some websites where I can learn more about Wraparound?

Wraparound services are now being offered nationwide and are one of the preferred programs for delivering treatment to austistic and special needs children. Below are some resources that you can use to keep abreast of changes, learn more about current procedures and find exciting, current, employment opportunities:

1. **National Wraparound Iniative**: Currently, Wraparound services are physician prescribed, but no national guidelines exist for how these programs are administered. NWI is an organization that works to develop inter-departmental relationships in an effort to standardize guidelines and support the overall development of quality programs. NWI's website offers current information on seminars and meetings being held nationwide, as well as some excellent publications that provide up-to-date descriptions of Wraparund services and autism treatment. www.rtc.pdx.edu/nwi

2. **Life - Watch**: Life-Watch is a healthcare employee assistance program that provides various benefits for healthcare professionals. This is an excellent resource to learn about autism, the various treatment methods and other valuable information on growing a career. www.lifewatch-eap.com

3. **MentalHelp.net**: This is an incredible site for anyone having trouble understanding Wraparound, autism, Pervasive Development Disorders and how these things fit into the larger mental healthcare industry. With sections on Wraparound and autism histories, this is an excellent place to start. www.mentalhelp.net

4. **AutismTreatmentINFO**: Aside from using this site for the information, an important part of building your career is finding resources to keep abreast of industry changes. There is a really good, free, newsletter that Autism Treatment Info puts out that is filled with important information. www.autismtreatment.info

Now, you might be wondering ....

1. What is a therapist (TSS)? **Page # 6**
94. What are some methods for autism treatment aside from ABA? **Page # 150**

QUESTION 96
What are some different roles that I can take in a career spent working with special needs children?

There are a number of different professional roles that you can take if you would like to work with special needs children. The following are some professional roles that you can fill when developing a career working with special needs children. Listed with these are some actual job descriptions written by hiring agencies:

1. Behavior Specialist

~The BSC is responsible for creating a behavior modification plan in conjunction with family members, teachers, and other individuals involved with the child.

~If the family or teachers are already using a behavior modification plan which is working successfully for the child, the BSC is responsible for utilizing the existing plan.

~The BSC assesses, designs, and monitors a program that fits the needs of each child and family, and is implemented in accordance with the Team's plan.

~The BSC is required to have obtained at least a Master's Degree.

2. Therapeutic Support Specialist / Therapist / TSS

~TSS workers provide one-on-one intervention with the client in the locations prescribed by the psychologist (home, school, and/or community).

~The TSS implements methods and interventions from the treatment plan to help the student achieve the goals of the treatment plan.

~TSS workers must keep their clients within eyesight at all times and are not permitted to conduct personal business or read while working with a client.

~During school hours the TSS does not just provide service during normal classes, they are with the client in the hallways, during lunch, recess, and special classes.

~TSS workers are required to have a college degree and experience working with children.

~Before working with a client for the first time TSS workers must complete over 30 hours of training. Each year the worker is required to have ongoing training to keep their skills up to date.

~All staff members are trained in Safe Crisis Management techniques, but are also trained to de-escalate situations so that they do not need to restrain a client in most circumstances.

~All staff members are committed to honoring the confidentiality of our clients and their families.

3. Mobile Therapist

~Mobile Therapists provide intensive therapeutic sessions for the child and family in non-traditional settings outside of the clinic or office.

~Mobile Therapists may meet with just the client or with the client and their family for a session.

~Mobile Therapy sessions vary according to the individualized needs of the client and their family members.

~Mobile Therapists are required to have attained at least a Master's Degree.

4. Case Manager

~Case managers are responsible for the administrative concerns related to providing treatment to clients. Along with the behavioral specialist, the case manager will meet with school officials, parents and healthcare providers to plan and coordinate treatment.

~The case manager is responsible for handling session scheduling, overseeing and deciding on the therapists that will conduct the interventions and fielding any problems that arise throughout the process.

Now, you might be wondering ....

1. What is a therapist (TSS)? **Page # 6**
2. What qualifications does a therapist need? **Page # 8**
3. What is a case manager? **Page # 9**
4. What qualifications does a case manager need? **Page # 10**
5. What is a behavioral specialist? **Page # 11**
6. What qualifications does a behavioral specialist need? **Page # 12**
7. What types of conflicts arise within a treatment team? **Page # 13**
8. What are the benefits in working with special needs children? **Page # 15**

What education is required for the different roles you can take in a career spent working with special needs children?

QUESTION 97

There are a number of different professional roles that you can take if you would like to work with special needs children. The following are some professional roles that you can fill when developing a career working with special needs children:

1. Psychologist - Though it is uncommon for a psychologist to actually administer treatment to a special needs child outside of a research environment, these professionals are responsible for overseeing treatment in many hospitals and clinics. The most important role of the psychologist is to guide a behavioral specialist when it comes to developing or altering treatment and also to make the initial diagnosis.

Most states require licensing to become a psychologist. In order to do this, you would need to pass the licensing exam and fullfill the educational requirements. With most programs, this means completing the necessary coursework and a doctoral dissertation. To learn more about entering this field, go to www.apa.org.

2. Behavior Specialist - A behavioral specialist is generally responsible for guiding the technical side of the treatment program. They develop the treatment plan, oversee client sessions, review data collected through sessions and make changes accordingly. Becoming a behavioral specialist requires a Master's Degree in the area of psychology, social work or education.

This is a good role to consider if your interests are more academic and you are pursuing or considering pursuing a doctoral degree.

3. Therapeutic Support Specialist or Therapist - A TSS or therapeutic specialist is the title for the professional that works one-on-one with the children in a treatment program. This position requires a Bachelor's of Science degree in social work, psychology or education. Since therapists tend to receive a great deal of training from the organization that employs them, there can be some variance with regards to educational requirements. Some experience working with children is almost always a requirement.

4. Case Manager - The case manager normally oversees the administrative concerns related to providing treatment. Educational requirements can vary, but a Master's Degree in psychology, social work, education or a related area can help in finding a position. Also, Case Manager certifications exist that will help you to find a position.

Now, you might be wondering ....

1. What is a therapist (TSS)? **Page # 6**

What are some fields I can pursue after getting experience working with special needs children?

One of the best things about working either as a therapist, case manager or behavioral specialist is that all of these professions build valuable skills that can be used in a number of fields. Also, given the required education, you will find that many opportunities exist that will not require extensive additional education.

Special Education Teaching and Administration

Many professionals who gained experience working with special needs children choose to move their career into the educational fields. With experience developing treatment plans, working with clients and coordinating with educational professionals, this is a great move for many individuals. Not only will you already have the experience necessary to work with children of special needs, but you can expand upon this work by addressing the educational requirements.

Mental Health Careers

When you work with special needs children, you are generally going to be working for a mental health care facility or organization. Though Wraparound and other programs are administered through social services, you are still using treatments and working within programs that were developed through studies related to Child Psychology. This type of experience can lead to other career fields in the area of mental health. Whether this means taking a position in a hospital, at a clinic or advancing your education to the point where you can treat patients through a psychiatric practice is entirely up to you. Regardless of the direction you choose, experience working with special needs children will help you to build skills that are frequently used throughout the mental health profession.

Criminal Justice System

Generally, 'special needs,' refers to children diagnosed with autism or one of the pervasive developmental disorders. However, when some people refer to special needs children, they also mean this to include children who have encountered experiences that made it necessary to place them within the juvenile justice system.

Regardless of whether you have spent time working with autistic children or a child that is moving through the juvenile justice system, these experiences can be of considerable use if you decided to move in the direction of criminal justice. The structure of a Wraparound program, with its involvement in coordinating individuals from schools, the community and family members, according to a predetermined system, is similar to the structure and methods used within the criminal justice system.

Other Careers

According to one therapist, the most important lessons she learned while working with autistic children was, "the ability to work as a member of a team in a well defined role." The fact that Wraparound, and other treatment programs, involve numerous professionals, each with a well defined role and purpose as a team member, will teach you the importance of teamwork - a skill that is greatly valued in almost any profession.

Now, you might be wondering ....

1. What is a therapist (TSS)? **Page # 6**
2. What qualifications does a therapist need? **Page # 8**
3. What is a case manager? **Page # 9**
4. What qualifications does a case manager need? **Page # 10**
5. What is a behavioral specialist? **Page # 11**
6. What qualifications does a behavioral specialist need? **Page # 12**
88. What organizations support careers involved in working with special needs children? **Page # 142**
89. What books are available to help me learn more about working with special needs children? **Page # 143**
90. What are some important moments in the history of autism treatment? **Page # 144**
91. Where can I find employment opportunities? **Page # 146**
92. Where can I find current information related to autism studies? **Page # 147**
93. What are some important moments in applied behavioral analysis? **Page # 148**

QUESTION 99

What are some notable organizations related to the history of working with special needs children?

Autism and the Pervasive Developmental Disorders are areas of study that fall within the larger field of Child Psychology, which is in turn just one area of the larger field of Psychology. The following organizations all relate in one way or another to these areas. Through the process of building a career spent working with special needs children, you will become acquainted in one way or another with these organizations:

1. **American Psychological Association** - There is an excellent page in the APA website for students that will give you access to a mentorship program and information on the many roles you can take when pursuing a career related to psychology. www.apa.org.

2. **The Autism Society of America** - This organization advocates for families and professionals who are concerned with autism. The organization frequently organizes seminars and meetings nationwide that are attended by representatives from organizations and other professionals that work in the field. A visit to their website will give you some more information about career opportunities and recent events in the world of autism research. www.autism-society.org.

3. **The Society for Research in Child Development** - Aside from the job opportunities posted on their website, this organization holds particular interest for anyone interested in careers related to working with autistic and PDD children. Their work is directly related to the disorders that a therapist encounters everyday. www.srcd.org.

4. **The Society for the Advancement of Behavioral Analysis** - This is a slightly smaller organization when compared to the others, but of noted importance to any professional involved in Wraparound or other programs that draw from Applied Behavioral Analysis. Involvement in SABA could be beneficial for someone that is especially interested in the science behind the treatment programs. www.abainternational.org.

Now, you might be wondering ....

88. What organizations support careers involved in working with special needs children? **Page # 142**
89. What books are available to help me learn more about working with special needs children? **Page # 143**
90. What are some important moments in the history of autism treatment? **Page # 144**

I think I want to work with special needs children, where should I start?

QUESTION 100

High School - Focus on the sciences. ABA and other autism treatment methods rely heavily on empirical science. Such topics as sociology, psychology and modern biology all will help you to take a role working with autistic children. At this stage in your education, it is very important to pay attention to the philosophy behind empirical sciences. Much of the therapy for autistic children involves recording hard data for later review. Understanding how the methods relate to the philosophy behind the science is absolutely necessary for a career in this field.

College - Aside from choosing a good school, you will want to work towards a degree related to psychology, sociology, education or social work. Many schools have begun to offer a master's degree track. In these types of programs you can work straight through to your master's degree, normally in only five years. This is a good way to approach your education, given that many of these positions require master's degrees and working through one program tends to make it much easier on a student.

Also, take labs! Any class that has you record and analyze data will be a major benefit. For most graduates just getting started in this field, developing the skills necessary to observe and record behaviors as hard data is the first hurdle. Taking labs that develop these skills will put you ahead of the game.

Internships - An internship involved with a Wraparound program is the best way to prepare for a job as a therapist, behaviorist or case manager, but it's not always necessary. Spending a few months interning at a hospital, educational facility or other child healthcare facility is a good way to prepare yourself and show potential employers that you are serious about pursuing this career field. What you'll need for most jobs is to show that you have worked with children and could handle the challenge.

Getting that First Job - There are a number of ways to get your first job. You'll find that getting your first job will most likely require a combination of networking, using your school career office, attending job fairs and directly applying to open positions. One good thing about working with special needs children is that once you have a little experience, you will find that there are many opportunities for employment and growth.

Now, you might be wondering ....

1. What is a therapist (TSS)? **Page # 6**

So - I've gone through this book. What's next?

You've gotten your questions answered. What do you do now?

Keep asking questions - Most people begin their education ,or even enter a profession, without ever having spoken to someone who is presently working in the field. Talking to a professor is a good place to start, but a bad place to stop. Take the time you have during your education to seek out people in the field, ask questions and get the information you need to make good decisions based on what's happening in the present.

Get experience at any cost - In a recent survey of employment recruiters, professionals said that beyond necessary qualifications, experience is the main factor they look at. Experience can mean more in today's job market than your school, grade point average or any other qualifying factors. It is also the only way to really know if you are going to enjoy the work that you do.

Getting experience *at any cost* is very important to being successful in your career. Understand that while you are in high school or college, employers see you more as a potential burden than an asset. Are you going to come to them as an intern and demand too much attention? Are you going to be argumentative or difficult to get along with? If you go to interview for an internship, reassure the person you speak with that you are there to help them in any way possible. Present yourself with professionalism and show them that you will work with them to meet their goals.

Don't give up - Ask any one who has built a successful career how they did it and most of them will tell you that it was nothing more than not giving up. There will always be someone with a higher G.P.A., with a degree from a better school, with better contacts and a wider network. This is true even if you graduated from Harvard with a 4.0. If it is what you want to do, then keep going. Keep getting experience *at any cost.* People are not born in a career. They find them.

Just keep asking questions, get experience and don't give up. AND - whether it is while working with special needs children or some other path, enjoy your career!

Good Luck!

About The 101 Series...

You've got career questions?

We've got career answers!

Every release in The 101 Career Questions Answered Series takes the questions that you've asked and gets them answered by experienced professionals.

Get information from insiders about important skills. Prepare for interviews and learn more about growing your career.

Whether you're just starting to think about college or already a member of the workforce, The 101 Career Questions Answered Series delivers straight answers to your important questions.

For more 101 Books visit us at:

www.laurellanepublishing.com

Don't Forget to Submit Your Childish Things Scholarship Essay and Application!

Every year, Laurel Lane, the publisher of The 101 Series, sponsors **The Childish Things Scholarship**. It's free to register and submit your essay.

The scholarship is open to all High School Seniors and any college student, with multiple awards, honorable mentions and in some cases publication of winning entries.

This scholarship is more than just a way to help you get money for your education. It is designed to help you prepare yourself for interviews, internships and your career.

For more information, rules and to apply, visit us at:

www.laurellanepublishing.com

Do You Own a Website?

Become an affiliate of one of the fastest growing book series in publishing today!

Our web affiliates generate a significant income based on customers referred to our website. Start making cash now!

Contact info@laurellanepublishing.com or visit our website at www.laurellanepublishing.com today for more information.

Check out these other books in

The 101 Career Questions Answered Series at www.laurellanepublishing.com

Your Career!
Being an Accountant
Working at a Nonprofit or Interest Group
Working in the Hospitality Industry
Being a Paralegal
Being a Broadcast News Reporter
Being a Television Producer
Working as an Information Technology Specialist
Being a High School Teacher
Being a College Professor
and
Many More to Come!